CROCK·POT®

· THE ORIGINAL SLOW COOKER ·

Skinny SLOW COOKER recipes

Publications International, Ltd.

Nutritional Analysis: Jacqueline B. Marcus, M.S., R.D., L.D., C.N.S., F.A.D.A.

Every effort has been made to check the accuracy of the nutritional information that appears with each recipe. However, because numerous variables account for a wide range of values for certain foods, nutritive analyses in this book should be consider approximate.

Pictured on the front cover: Curry Chicken with Mango and Red Pepper *(page 148).*
Pictured on the back cover: Pork and Tomato Ragoût *(page 134).*

ISBN-13: 978-1-4508-8121-0

Manufactured in China.

8 7 6 5 4 3 2 1

Contents

Healthy Eating

Many families look for ways to balance their need to eat healthful, nutritious meals with their desire to eat the hearty, home-style food most familiar to them. This book presents a solution: healthful versions of classic comfort foods made in the **CROCK-POT®** slow cooker.

Eating together at home as a family can nurture relationships and promote quality time. In addition, cooking at home allows you to choose your ingredients and control your portions. The familiar, well-loved recipes in this book prove that you can prepare and eat healthy food without sacrificing good taste. Even better, you can count on your **CROCK-POT®** slow cooker to create the same time-tested, convenient, and hassle-free meals it always has.

Whether you're embarking on a new healthy eating plan, or you're looking for some nutritious recipes to add to your repertoire, this book has something for you. The recipes were selected to offer delicious, nutritionally balanced foods that cooks everywhere can confidently offer to their families.

The Principles of Healthy Eating

Whether you're trying to lose weight, maintain your weight, or just eat better, basic nutrition information is what you need under your belt. It's easy to be led astray and ultimately become disappointed by misinformation and diets that make outrageous promises. That's why it is important to learn about the role of nutrients in food and how these nutrients are used in your body. Armed with this knowledge, you can resist the siren call of unhealthy diets and make an informed decision about a healthy eating plan that's right for you.

Nutrition Fundamentals

Most foods contain a combination of three energy-producing nutrients—protein, fat, and carbohydrate. These nutrients are responsible for providing the energy that your body's engine needs to run well, and they are essential to your health. Your body requires all three, as well as vitamins, minerals, and water. Fiber, a type of carbohydrate, and fluids both play important roles in managing your weight, too.

If you're trying to lose weight, you've certainly heard the word calorie. Basically, calorie is another word for energy. There are four sources of calories: the three energy-producing nutrients mentioned above (protein, fat, and carbohydrate) and alcohol. Fiber, although it's a carbohydrate, is not processed by the body and is calorie-free.

Calorie Basics

Weight loss (and weight gain, for that matter) is primarily an issue of calories: how many you consume and how many you expend. If the number of calories you eat and the number of calories you use each day are approximately the same, your weight won't budge. It's

only when you consume fewer calories than you use over a period of time that you will lose weight. And it's only when you eat more calories than you use that you will gain weight.

So what numbers of calories are we talking about? This is the crucial equation: One pound of body weight is equal to 3,500 calories. This means that to lose one pound, you must create a 3,500-calorie shortage by eating fewer calories, burning more calories through physical activity, or a combination of both. The exact opposite is true for weight gain. Sounds like a lot, doesn't it? But it's not really. Gaining a pound is as easy as eating an extra 250 calories a day (for instance, any of these: three chocolate chip cookies, one milk chocolate bar, two ounces Cheddar cheese, or a medium-size bagel) for two weeks or skipping a daily workout without cutting back on eating.

And despite claims from popular diet plans, a calorie is a calorie, whether it comes from protein, fat, or carbohydrate. Any calories eaten that your body doesn't burn for energy are stored as body fat, no matter what kind of food package they came in.

There are a few other factors, in addition to calories, that influence your weight. They are your age, your gender, and your genetic blueprint. Unfortunately, these factors are out of your control. So focus on food intake and physical activity, the areas in which you can have an impact.

Making Smart Choices

Eating right and being physically active go hand in hand with keeping a healthy lifestyle. There are certain guidelines you should follow to keep on top of your healthy habits and reducing your risk of chronic diseases and obesity.

The best way to get a handle on eating right is to balance your meals by eating a variety of foods each day. Your goal should be to:

- Select lean sources of protein—like lean meats and poultry. Also add more fish, beans, legumes, and nuts for additional protein.
- Select fresh fruits and vegetables when you can. Opt for fresh, frozen, canned, or dried fruits over fruit juices and choose more dark green or orange vegetables for added nutrition and increased fiber.
- Make half your grains whole. Choose whole grains when possible, when selecting cereals, breads, rice, and pasta. Look for grains that say "whole grains" in the ingredient list. This will also be a fiber boost for you.
- Choose fat-free and low-fat milk and dairy products, like cheese and yogurt. These foods will provide you with all that great nutrition, but without excess fat.

- Know your limits. Look for foods that are low in saturated fats, trans fats, cholesterol, salt (sodium), and added sugars.

Each person should aim for a certain number of calories each day. This particular number is based on your age, sex, activity level, and whether you are seeking to maintain your weight, gain weight, or lose weight. Typically 2,000 calories is the general reference number used for the average adult to maintain their weight. If you are seeking to lose a few pounds, you will need to reduce this number of calories.

When choosing foods, whether they be those for meals or for snacks, you should seek out choices that are "nutrient dense" and not "empty-calorie" foods. In other words, you should choose foods that provide you the most nutrition for the number of calories (or food energy) that they provide. Choosing foods with calories as well as adequate vitamins and minerals would definitely be a better choice than one, like a sugary soft drink, that provides only calories from sugar, and no other nutrition value.

Healthy Eating

Now that you are focusing on the "better" choices, you must also keep in mind the importance of portion sizes. Any food that is eaten in too large a quantity, even a good-for-you food, is not a good choice. In order to balance your meals, you should seek out the variety of foods you need, in recommended portion sizes. Refer to the chart below for some examples.

The Comfort of Food

The process of improving one's diet can seem fairly daunting, even frightening. We hear and see so many messages on the importance of a healthful diet that it's easy to feel overwhelmed by the decision of what to eat.

Partly this is because many of the messages we receive about food conflict with one another. But another key factor is the role food plays in our lives.

On a certain level, food plays a basic functional role in our daily lives. There are plenty of scientific studies documenting how many calories a person needs each day, the best sources of those calories, the sorts of nutrients we need to ingest each day, etc. While we certainly need to fuel our bodies, food means much more to us than just fuel. Food provides a much needed emotional contact for most people. A shared dinner is the centerpiece of many families' daily interactions with one another. Comfort food comforts us in these and many other ways.

Choose Wisely

Eating the familiar, well-loved recipes in this book can help you keep to a sensible eating plan. Consider the following ways to help create healthier versions of your own favorite CROCK-POT® slow cooker recipes.

In general

- Portion sizes are incredibly important. Don't be afraid to measure out portions with measuring cups or an accurate kitchen scale.
- Use high calorie or fatty ingredients sparingly or as garnish. Try sprinkling cheese on top of each serving, rather than adding cups of it into the recipe itself. You'll still get the flavor, but you'll avoid all of the fat.

Ingredients are important

- Recipes using leaner cuts of meat are great choices to start with. Look for recipes for skinless, boneless white meat cuts of poultry. Beef recipes made with cuts with "loin" or "round" in their names are also good options, as are pork recipes made with boneless "loin" cuts.
- Try substituting equal weights of these boneless cuts for bone-in or fattier cuts in your favorite recipes.
- Look for reduced-fat and reduced-sodium versions of other commonly used ingredients. For example, almost all of the canned broths and canned beans used in these recipes are either reduced-fat or reduced-sodium versions.
- Packaged and prepared products are convenient, but they are often the source of hidden salt or fat in recipes. Try fresh or frozen alternatives to boxed or canned versions whenever practical.

Relative Serving Sizes

There will be occasions when it may be difficult or impractical to measure your meals with a scale or measuring cups. Learning how to estimate appropriate serving sizes can be tricky, but it's made easier if you learn to approximate relative sizes like those in this list:

Fruits
1 cup cut-up fruit = closed fist
½ cup grapes or berries = light bulb
1 medium apple, orange, pear, etc. = baseball

Vegetables
1 cup baby carrots = tennis ball
1 medium ear of corn = as long as an unsharpened pencil
1 cup broccoli florets = rounded handful

Dairy
1 ounce firm cheese (like Cheddar) = 9-volt battery
1 cup yogurt or cottage cheese = closed fist

½ cup shredded cheese = enough to fill a typical paper cupcake liner

Proteins
3 ounces beef or pork = deck of cards or about the size of the palm of your hand
3 ounces chicken = average size chicken leg and thigh portion; small chicken breast
3 ounces grilled or baked fish fillet = checkbook

Grains and Starches
½ cup pasta or rice = typical scoop of ice cream
1 ounce bread = typical slice of sandwich bread
1 medium potato = computer mouse

What Is Comfort Food?

When we connect with our loved ones over specific foods, those foods take on an emotional weight of their own. That's why, even years later Grandma's special Sunday roast recipe reminds us of her and the good times we shared with the whole family. That's one of the most important ways certain foods, comfort foods especially, feed our emotional sides in addition to our physical sides.

For most Americans, "comfort foods" include many of the most classic sorts of **CROCK-POT**® slow cooker foods like pot roast, roasted chicken and potatoes, chicken soup and even spicier fare like chili. Unfortunately, some of the traditional ways of cooking these recipes rely on unhealthy levels of fat and sodium to create the great flavors we remember.

Comfort Food = Diet Food?

The recipes in this book were selected to have fewer calories, fat, sodium, and cholesterol than typical comfort-food recipes. Consider your own dietary needs and calorie allowance for the day when choosing recipes. Refer to the nutritional analysis for each recipe so you have the information to select the recipes that are appropriate for you.

With this book it's simple to plan meals and budget your calories. For example, if you have a higher calorie lunch, select a dinner that's lower in calories to balance out your intake.

Whether you're trying to lose weight, hoping to prevent gaining additional weight, or just looking for ways to eat healthier, the recipes in this book can provide you the heart-warming comfort of your favorite foods, without the fat and calories.

The Joy of Slow Cooking

Slow Cooker Hints and Tips

Slow Cooker Sizes

Smaller slow cookers—such as 1- to 3$\frac{1}{2}$-quart models—are the perfect size for cooking for singles, a couple, or empty-nesters (and also for serving dips).

While medium-size slow cookers (those holding somewhere between 3 quarts and 5 quarts) will easily cook enough food at a time to feed a small family, they're also convenient for holiday side dishes or appetizers.

Large slow cookers are great for large family dinners, holiday entertaining, and potluck suppers. A 6-quart to 7-quart model is ideal if you like to make meals in advance, or have dinner tonight and store leftovers for another day.

Types of Slow Cookers

Current **CROCK-POT®** slow cookers come equipped with many different features and benefits, from auto cook programs to stovetop-safe stoneware to timed programming. Visit **www.crock-pot.com** to find the slow cooker that best suits your needs.

How you plan to use a slow cooker may affect the model you choose to purchase. For everyday cooking, choose a size large enough to serve your family. If you plan to use the slow cooker primarily for entertaining, choose one of the larger sizes. Basic slow cookers can hold as little as 16 ounces or as much as 7 quarts. The smallest sizes are great for keeping dips hot on a buffet, while the larger sizes can more readily fit large quantities of food and larger roasts.

Cooking, Stirring, and Food Safety

CROCK-POT® slow cookers are safe to leave unattended. The outer heating base may get hot as it cooks, but it should not pose a fire hazard. The heating element in the heating base functions at a low wattage and is safe for your countertops.

The Joy of Slow Cooking

Your slow cooker should be filled about one-half to three-fourths full for most recipes unless otherwise instructed. Lean meats such as chicken or pork tenderloin will cook faster than meats with more connective tissue and fat such as beef chuck or pork shoulder. Bone-in meats will take longer than boneless cuts. Typical slow cooker dishes take approximately 7 to 8 hours to reach the simmer point on LOW and about 3 to 4 hours on HIGH. Once the vegetables and meat start to simmer and braise, their flavors will fully blend and meat will become fall-off-the-bone tender.

According to the USDA, all bacteria are killed at a temperature of 165°F. It's important to follow the recommended cooking times and not to open the lid often, especially early in the cooking process when heat is building up inside the unit. If you need to open the lid to check on your food or are adding additional ingredients, remember to allow additional cooking time if necessary to ensure food is cooked through and tender.

Large slow cookers, the 6- to 7-quart sizes, may benefit with a quick stir halfway during cook time to help distribute heat and promote even cooking. It's usually unnecessary to stir at all, as even $1/2$ cup liquid will help to distribute heat, and the stoneware is the perfect medium for holding food at an even temperature throughout the cooking process.

Oven-Safe

All **CROCK-POT**® slow cooker removable stoneware inserts may (without their lids) be used safely in ovens at up to 400°F. Also, all **CROCK-POT**® slow cookers are microwavable without their lids. If you own another brand slow cooker, please refer to your owner's manual for specific stoneware cooking medium tolerances.

Frozen Food

Frozen food or partially frozen food can be successfully cooked in a slow cooker; however, it will require longer cooking than the same recipe made with fresh food. It's almost always preferable to thaw frozen food prior to placing it in the slow cooker. Using an instant-read thermometer is recommended to ensure meat is fully cooked through.

Pasta and Rice

If you're converting a recipe that calls for uncooked pasta, cook the pasta on the stovetop just until slightly tender before adding to the slow cooker. If you are converting a recipe that calls for cooked rice, stir in raw rice with other ingredients; add 1/4 cup extra liquid per 1/4 cup of raw rice.

Beans

Beans must be softened completely before combining with sugar and/or acidic foods. Sugar and acid have a hardening effect on beans and will prevent softening. Fully cooked canned beans may be used as a substitute for dried beans.

Vegetables

Root vegetables often cook more slowly than meat. Cut vegetables accordingly to cook at the same rate as meat—

The Joy of Slow Cooking

large or small, or lean versus marbled—and place near the sides or bottom of the stoneware to facilitate cooking.

Herbs

Fresh herbs add flavor and color when added at the end of the cooking cycle; if added at the beginning, many fresh herbs' flavor will dissipate over long cook times. Ground and/or dried herbs and spices work well in slow cooking and may be added at the beginning, and for dishes with shorter cook times, hearty fresh herbs such as rosemary and thyme hold up well. The flavor power of all herbs and spices can vary greatly depending on their particular strength and shelf life. Use chili powders and garlic powder sparingly, as these can sometimes intensify over the long cook times. Always taste the dish at end of the cook cycle and correct seasonings including salt and pepper.

Liquids

It's not necessary to use more than ½ to 1 cup liquid in most instances since juices in meats and vegetables are retained more in slow cooking than in conventional cooking. Excess liquid can be cooked down and concentrated after slow cooking on the stovetop or by removing meat and vegetables from the stoneware, stirring in one of the following thickeners, and setting the slow cooker to HIGH. Cook on HIGH for approximately 15 minutes until juices are thickened.

Flour: All-purpose flour is often used to thicken soups or stews. Place flour in a small bowl or cup and stir in enough cold water to make a thin, lump-free mixture. With the slow cooker on HIGH, quickly whisk the flour mixture into the liquid in the slow cooker. Cook, stirring frequently, until the mixture thickens.

Cornstarch: Cornstarch gives sauces a clear, shiny appearance; it's used most often for sweet dessert sauces and stir-fry sauces. Place cornstarch in a small bowl or cup and stir in cold water, stirring until the cornstarch dissolves. Quickly whisk this mixture into the liquid in the slow cooker; the sauce will thicken as soon as the liquid boils. Cornstarch breaks down with too much heat, so never add it at the beginning of the slow cooking process, and turn off the heat as soon as the sauce thickens.

Arrowroot: Arrowroot (or arrowroot flour) comes from the root of a tropical plant that is dried and ground to a powder; it produces a thick clear sauce. Those who are allergic to wheat often use it in place of flour. Place arrowroot in a small bowl or cup and stir in cold water until the mixture is smooth. Quickly whisk this mixture into the liquid in the slow cooker. Arrowroot thickens below the boiling point, so it even works well in a slow cooker on LOW. Too much stirring can break down an arrowroot mixture.

Tapioca: Tapioca is a starchy substance extracted from the root of the cassava plant. Its greatest advantage is that it withstands long cooking, making it an ideal choice for slow cooking. Add it at the beginning of cooking and you'll get a clear thickened sauce in the finished dish. Dishes using tapioca as a thickener are best cooked on the LOW setting; tapioca may become stringy when boiled for a long time.

Milk

Milk, cream, and sour cream break down during extended cooking. When possible, add during the last 15 to 30 minutes of cooking, just until heated through. Condensed soups may be substituted for milk and can cook for extended times.

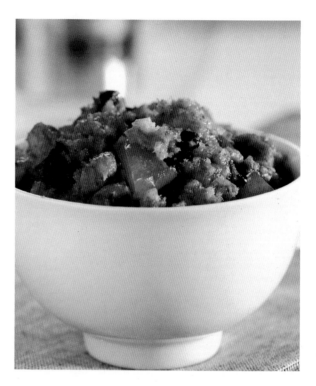

Fish

Fish is delicate and should be stirred in gently during the last 15 to 30 minutes of cooking time. Cook until just cooked through and serve immediately.

Baked Goods

If you wish to prepare bread, cakes, or pudding cakes in a slow cooker, you may want to purchase a covered, vented metal cake pan accessory for your slow cooker. You can also use any straight-sided soufflé dish or deep cake pan that will fit into the stoneware insert of your unit. Baked goods can be prepared directly in the insert; however, they can be a little difficult to remove from the insert, so follow the recipe directions carefully.

Breakfast

Apple-Cinnamon Breakfast Risotto

- **3 tablespoons unsalted butter**
- **4 medium Granny Smith apples (about 1½ pounds), peeled and cut into ½-inch cubes**
- **1½ teaspoons ground cinnamon**
- **¼ teaspoon ground allspice**
- **¼ teaspoon salt**
- **1½ cups uncooked Arborio rice**
- **½ cup packed dark brown sugar**
- **4 cups unfiltered apple juice, at room temperature***
- **1 teaspoon vanilla**
- **Optional toppings: dried cranberries, sliced almonds and/or milk**

***If unfiltered apple juice is unavailable, use any apple juice.**

1. Coat inside of **CROCK-POT®** slow cooker with nonstick cooking spray. Melt butter in large skillet over medium-high heat. Add apples, cinnamon, allspice and salt; cook and stir 3 to 5 minutes or until apples begin to release juices. Remove to **CROCK-POT®** slow cooker.

2. Stir in rice and sprinkle evenly with brown sugar. Add apple juice and vanilla. Cover; cook on HIGH 1½ to 2 hours or until all liquid is absorbed. Top as desired.

Makes 6 servings

Nutrition Information: Serving Size about 1¼ cups, Calories 342, Total Fat 6g, Saturated Fat 4g, Protein 2g, Carbohydrate 72g, Cholesterol 15mg, Dietary Fiber 4g, Sodium 123mg

Bran Muffin Bread

>   2 **cups all-bran cereal**
>   2 **cups whole wheat flour***
>   2 **teaspoons baking powder**
>   1 **teaspoon baking soda**
>   ¼ **teaspoon ground cinnamon**
>   ½ **teaspoon salt**
>   1 **egg**
> 1½ **cups buttermilk**
>   ¼ **cup molasses**
>   ¼ **cup (½ stick) unsalted butter, melted**
>   1 **cup chopped walnuts**
>   ½ **cup raisins**
>   **Prepared honey butter (optional)**

For proper texture of finished bread, spoon flour into measuring cup and level off. Do not dip into bag, pack down flour or tap on counter to level when measuring.

1. Butter and flour 8-cup mold that fits inside 6-quart **CROCK-POT®** slow cooker. Combine cereal, flour, baking powder, baking soda, cinnamon and salt in large bowl.

2. Beat egg in medium bowl. Whisk in buttermilk, molasses and melted butter. Stir into flour mixture just until combined. Stir in walnuts and raisins. Spoon batter into prepared mold. Cover with buttered foil, butter side down.

3. Place rack in **CROCK-POT®** slow cooker. Pour 1 inch hot water into **CROCK-POT®** slow cooker (water should not come to top of rack). Place mold on rack. Cover; cook on LOW 3½ to 4 hours or until bread starts to pull away from side of mold and toothpick inserted into center comes out clean. (If necessary, replace foil. Cover; cook on LOW 45 minutes.)

4. Remove mold from **CROCK-POT®** slow cooker. Let stand 10 minutes. Remove foil and run rubber spatula around outer edge, lifting bottom slightly to loosen. Invert bread onto wire rack. Serve warm with honey butter, if desired.

Makes 1 loaf

Nutrition Information: Serving Size 1 slice (1/12 loaf), Calories 258, Total Fat 12g, Saturated Fat 4g, Protein 8g, Carbohydrate 36g, Cholesterol 31mg, Dietary Fiber 6g, Sodium 356mg

Orange Date Nut Bread

2 **cups all-purpose flour, plus additional for dusting**

½ **cup chopped pecans**

1 **teaspoon baking powder**

½ **teaspoon baking soda**

¼ **teaspoon salt**

1 **cup chopped dates**

2 **teaspoons orange peel**

⅔ **cup boiling water**

¾ **cup sugar**

2 **tablespoons shortening**

1 **egg, lightly beaten**

1 **teaspoon vanilla**

Variation
Substitute 1 cup dried cranberries for dates.

1. Spray 1-quart casserole, soufflé dish or other high-sided baking dish with nonstick cooking spray; dust with flour.

2. Combine 2 cups flour, pecans, baking powder, baking soda and salt in medium bowl.

3. Combine dates and orange peel in separate medium bowl; pour boiling water over date mixture. Add sugar, shortening, egg and vanilla; stir just until blended.

4. Add flour mixture to date mixture; stir just until blended. Pour batter into prepared dish; place in 4½-quart **CROCK-POT®** slow cooker. Cover; cook on HIGH 2½ hours or until edge begins to brown.

5. Remove dish from **CROCK-POT®** slow cooker. Cool on wire rack 10 minutes. Remove bread from dish; cool completely on rack.

Makes 10 servings

Nutrition Information: Serving Size 1 slice (¹⁄₁₀ loaf), Calories 365, Total Fat 7g, Saturated Fat 1g, Protein 8g, Carbohydrate 48g, Cholesterol 22mg, Dietary Fiber 2g, Sodium 490mg

Breakfast

Ham and Cheddar Brunch Strata

8 ounces French bread, torn into small pieces

1¾ cups (7 ounces) shredded reduced-fat sharp Cheddar cheese, divided

1 cup diced lean ham

½ cup finely chopped green onions (white and green parts), divided

4 eggs

1 cup fat-free half-and-half

1 tablespoon Worcestershire sauce

⅛ teaspoon ground red pepper

Tip

When preparing ingredients for the **CROCK-POT®** slow cooker, cut into uniform pieces so everything cooks evenly.

1. Coat inside of **CROCK-POT®** slow cooker with nonstick cooking spray. Cut waxed paper to fit bottom of stoneware; press into place.* Spray paper with nonstick cooking spray. Layer bread, 1½ cups cheese, ham and 6 tablespoons green onions in **CROCK-POT®** slow cooker.

2. Whisk eggs, half-and-half, Worcestershire sauce and ground red pepper in small bowl; pour evenly into **CROCK-POT®** slow cooker. Cover; cook on LOW 3½ hours or until knife inserted into center comes out clean. Turn off heat. Sprinkle evenly with remaining ¼ cup cheese and 2 tablespoons green onions. Let stand, covered, 10 minutes or until cheese is melted.

3. To serve, run knife or rubber spatula around outer edge, lifting bottom slightly. Invert onto plate; peel off paper. Invert again onto large serving plate.

To cut waxed paper, trace around the stoneware bottom, then cut the paper slightly smaller to fit.

Makes 8 servings

Nutrition Information: Serving Size about 1 cup, Calories 273, Total Fat 10g, Saturated Fat 4g, Protein 19g, Carbohydrate 28g, Cholesterol 142mg, Dietary Fiber 1g, Sodium 562mg

Glazed Orange Poppy Seed Cake

Batter

- 1½ cups biscuit baking mix
- ¾ cup granulated sugar
- 2 tablespoons poppy seeds
- ½ cup sour cream
- 1 egg
- 2 tablespoons reduced-fat (2%) milk
- 1 teaspoon vanilla
- 2 teaspoons orange peel

Glaze

- ¼ cup orange juice
- 2 cups powdered sugar
- 2 teaspoons poppy seeds

1. Coat inside of 4-quart **CROCK-POT®** slow cooker with nonstick cooking spray. Cut waxed paper to fit bottom of stoneware; press into place.* Spray paper lightly with nonstick cooking spray.

2. Combine baking mix, granulated sugar and 2 tablespoons poppy seeds in medium bowl; stir to blend. Combine sour cream, egg, milk, vanilla and orange peel in medium bowl. Stir sour cream mixture into baking mix mixture until well blended.

3. Spoon batter into **CROCK-POT®** slow cooker; smooth top. Place paper towel under lid. Cover; cook on HIGH 1 hour 30 minutes or until toothpick inserted into center comes out clean.

4. Invert onto wire rack with clean waxed paper underneath. Peel off waxed paper; cool completely.

5. Whisk orange juice into powdered sugar in small bowl. Cut cake into eight wedges. Spread glaze with spatula over top and sides of each wedge. Sprinkle 2 teaspoons poppy seeds over wedges and allow glaze to set.

Makes 8 servings

To cut waxed paper, trace around the stoneware bottom, then cut the paper slightly smaller to fit.

Nutrition Information: Serving Size 1 slice (⅛ cake), Calories 342, Total Fat 7g, Saturated Fat 3g, Protein 4g, Carbohydrate 66g, Cholesterol 37mg, Dietary Fiber 0g, Sodium 475mg

Glazed Cinnamon Coffee Cake

Streusel

- ¼ **cup biscuit baking mix**
- ¼ **cup packed light brown sugar**
- ½ **teaspoon ground cinnamon**

Batter

- 1½ **cups biscuit baking mix**
- ¾ **cup granulated sugar**
- ½ **cup unflavored yogurt**
- 1 **egg, lightly beaten**
- 1 **teaspoon vanilla**

Glaze

- 2 **tablespoons reduced-fat (2%) milk**
- 1 **cup powdered sugar**
- ½ **cup sliced almonds (optional)**

Note
This recipe works best in a round **CROCK-POT®** slow cooker.

1. Coat inside of 4-quart **CROCK-POT®** slow cooker with nonstick cooking spray.

2. Prepare streusel: Blend ¼ cup baking mix, brown sugar and cinnamon in small bowl; set aside.

3. Prepare batter: Mix 1½ cups baking mix, granulated sugar, yogurt, egg and vanilla in medium bowl until well blended. Spoon half of batter into **CROCK-POT®** slow cooker. Sprinkle half of streusel over top. Repeat with remaining batter and streusel.

4. Line lid with two paper towels. Cover tightly; cook on HIGH 1¾ to 2 hours or until toothpick inserted into center comes out clean and cake springs back when gently pressed. Turn off heat. Allow cake to rest 10 minutes. Invert onto serving plate.

5. Prepare glaze: Whisk milk into powdered sugar in small bowl, 1 tablespoon at a time, until desired consistency. Spoon glaze over top of cake. Garnish with almonds. Cut into wedges. Serve warm or cold.

Makes 8 servings

Nutrition Information: Serving Size 1 slice (⅛ cake), Calories 283, Total Fat 4g, Saturated Fat 1g, Protein 4g, Carbohydrate 60g, Cholesterol 28mg, Dietary Fiber 0g, Sodium 404mg

Breakfast

Whole-Grain Banana Bread

- ¼ **cup plus 2 tablespoons wheat germ, divided**
- 1 **cup sugar**
- ½ **cup (1 stick) unsalted light butter, softened**
- 2 **eggs**
- 3 **medium bananas, mashed (about 1 cup)**
- 1 **teaspoon vanilla**
- 1 **cup all-purpose flour**
- 1 **cup whole wheat pastry flour**
- ½ **cup chopped walnuts or pecans (optional)**
- 1 **teaspoon baking soda**
- ½ **teaspoon salt**

1. Spray 1-quart casserole that fits into 4½-quart **CROCK-POT®** slow cooker with nonstick cooking spray. Sprinkle dish with 2 tablespoons wheat germ.

2. Beat sugar and butter in large bowl with electric mixer at medium speed 2 minutes or until fluffy. Add eggs, one at a time, beating well after each addition. Add bananas and vanilla; beat 2 minutes or until smooth. Stir in flours, nuts, if desired, remaining ¼ cup wheat germ, baking soda and salt; pour batter into prepared dish. Place in **CROCK-POT®** slow cooker.

3. Cover; cook on LOW 4 to 6 hours or on HIGH 2 to 3 hours or until edges begin to brown and toothpick inserted into center comes out clean. Remove casserole from **CROCK-POT®** slow cooker. Cool on wire rack 10 minutes. Invert bread onto wire rack; cool completely.

Makes 10 servings

Nutrition Information: Serving Size 1 slice (¹⁄₁₀ loaf), Calories 285, Total Fat 8g, Saturated Fat 4g, Protein 6g, Carbohydrate 49g, Cholesterol 55mg, Dietary Fiber 4g, Sodium 419mg

Breakfast

Cheese Grits with Chiles and Bacon

  3 slices turkey bacon, divided

  1 jalapeño pepper, seeded and minced*

  1 small yellow onion, finely chopped

  1 cup grits**

  4 cups 99% fat-free sodium-free chicken broth

¼ teaspoon salt

¼ teaspoon black pepper

  1 cup (4 ounces) shredded reduced-fat sharp Cheddar cheese

½ cup fat-free half-and-half

  2 tablespoons finely chopped green onion (green part only)

*Jalapeño peppers can sting and irritate the skin, so wear rubber gloves when handling peppers and do not touch your eyes.

**You may use coarse, instant, yellow or stone-ground grits.

1. Heat medium skillet over medium heat. Add bacon; cook and stir until crisp. Drain on paper towels. Crumble 2 slices and place in **CROCK-POT®** slow cooker. Crumble and refrigerate remaining 1 slice bacon.

2. Drain all but 1 tablespoon bacon drippings from skillet. Add jalapeño pepper and onion; cook and stir over medium–high heat 1 minute or until onion is lightly browned. Remove to **CROCK-POT®** slow cooker. Stir in grits, broth, salt and black pepper. Cover; cook on LOW 4 hours.

3. Stir in cheese and half-and-half. Sprinkle each serving with green onion and reserved bacon.

Makes 4 servings

Nutrition Information: Serving Size about 1¼ cups, Calories 305, Total Fat 11g, Saturated Fat 5g, Protein 8g, Carbohydrate 6g, Cholesterol 60mg, Dietary Fiber 1g, Sodium 605mg

Breakfast

Breakfast Berry Bread Pudding

- **6 cups bread, preferably dense peasant-style or sourdough, cut into ¾- to 1-inch cubes**
- **1 cup raisins**
- **½ cup slivered almonds, toasted***
- **6 eggs, beaten**
- **1¾ cups low-fat (1%) milk**
- **1½ cups packed brown sugar**
- **1½ teaspoons ground cinnamon**
- **1 teaspoon vanilla**
- **3 cups sliced fresh strawberries**
- **2 cups fresh blueberries**

*To toast almonds, spread in single layer in heavy skillet. Cook over medium heat 1 to 2 minutes or until nuts are lightly browned, stirring frequently.

1. Coat inside of **CROCK-POT®** slow cooker with nonstick cooking spray. Add bread, raisins and almonds; toss to combine.

2. Whisk eggs, milk, brown sugar, cinnamon and vanilla in large bowl. Pour egg mixture over bread mixture; stir to coat. Cover; cook on LOW 4 to 4½ hours or on HIGH 3 hours.

3. Remove stoneware from **CROCK-POT®** slow cooker. Let bread pudding cool until set. Serve with berries.

Makes 12 servings

Nutrition Information: Serving Size about 1 cup, Calories 300, Total Fat 6g, Saturated Fat 1g, Protein 7g, Carbohydrate 57g, Cholesterol 109mg, Dietary Fiber 3g, Sodium 179mg

Honey Whole-Grain Bread

3 cups whole wheat bread flour, divided

2 cups warm (not hot) whole milk

³/₄ cup all-purpose flour, divided

¹/₄ cup honey

2 tablespoons vegetable oil

1 package active dry yeast

³/₄ teaspoon salt

1. Make foil handles using three 18 × 2-inch strips of heavy-duty foil or use regular foil folded to double thickness. Place in stoneware; crisscross foil to form spoke design across bottom and up sides. Spray 1-quart casserole that fits in 4¹/₂-quart **CROCK-POT®** slow cooker with nonstick cooking spray.

2. Combine 1¹/₂ cups whole wheat flour, milk, ¹/₂ cup all-purpose flour, honey, oil, yeast and salt in large bowl. Beat with electric mixer at medium speed 2 minutes. Add remaining 1¹/₂ cups whole wheat flour and ¹/₄ cup to ¹/₂ cup all-purpose flour until dough is no longer sticky. Remove to prepared casserole.

3. Place casserole in **CROCK-POT®** slow cooker. Cover; cook on HIGH 3 hours or until edges are browned. Use foil handles to lift dish from **CROCK-POT®** slow cooker. Let stand 5 minutes. Invert onto wire rack; cool completely.

Makes 10 servings

Nutrition Information: Serving Size 1 slice (¹/₁₀ loaf), Calories 237, Total Fat 5g, Saturated Fat 1g, Protein 8g, Carbohydrate 42g, Cholesterol 5mg, Dietary Fiber 5g, Sodium 316mg

Whoa Breakfast

3 cups water

2 cups chopped peeled apples

1½ cups steel-cut or old-fashioned oats

¼ cup sliced almonds

½ teaspoon ground cinnamon

Combine water, apples, oats, almonds and cinnamon in **CROCK-POT®** slow cooker; stir well. Cover; cook on LOW 8 hours.

Makes 6 servings

Nutrition Information: Serving Size about 1 cup, Calories 124, Total Fat 3g, Saturated Fat 0g, Protein 4g, Carbohydrate 20g, Cholesterol 0mg, Dietary Fiber 4g, Sodium 5mg

Hawaiian Fruit Compote

3 cups coarsely chopped fresh pineapple

3 grapefruits, peeled and sectioned

1 can (21 ounces) cherry pie filling

2 cups chopped fresh peaches

2 to 3 limes, peeled and sectioned

1 mango, peeled and chopped

2 bananas, peeled and sliced

1 tablespoon lemon juice

Slivered almonds (optional)

Serving Suggestions

Try warm, fruity compote in place of maple syrup on your favorite pancakes or waffles for a great way to start your day. This sauce is also delicious served over roasted turkey, pork roast or baked ham.

Place pineapple, grapefruits, cherry pie filling, peaches, limes, mango, bananas and lemon juice in **CROCK-POT**® slow cooker; toss lightly. Cover; cook on LOW 4 to 5 hours or on HIGH 2 to 3 hours. Serve with slivered almonds, if desired.

Makes 8 servings

Nutrition Information: Serving Size about 1 cup, Calories 225, Total Fat 0g, Saturated Fat 0g, Protein 2g, Carbohydrate 58g, Cholesterol 0mg, Dietary Fiber 8g, Sodium 15mg

Breakfast

Mucho Mocha Cocoa

1 cup chocolate syrup

⅓ cup instant coffee granules

2 tablespoons sugar

1 teaspoon ground cinnamon

1 quart reduced-fat (2%) milk

1 quart fat-free half-and-half

Combine chocolate syrup, coffee granules, sugar, cinnamon, milk and half-and-half in **CROCK-POT®** slow cooker; stir until well blended. Cover; cook on LOW 3 hours. Serve warm in mugs.

Makes 9 servings

Nutrition Information: Serving Size about 1 cup, Calories 229, Total Fat 4g, Saturated Fat 2g, Protein 7g, Carbohydrate 41g, Cholesterol 14mg, Dietary Fiber 1g, Sodium 230mg

Pear Crunch

1 **can (8 ounces) crushed pineapple in juice, undrained**

¼ **cup pineapple or apple juice**

3 **tablespoons dried cranberries**

1½ **teaspoons quick-cooking tapioca**

¼ **teaspoon vanilla**

2 **pears, cored and cut into halves**

¼ **cup granola with almonds**

Fresh mint leaves (optional)

1. Combine pineapple, juice, cranberries, tapioca and vanilla in **CROCK-POT®** slow cooker; mix well. Place pears cut side down on pineapple mixture.

2. Cover; cook on LOW 3½ to 4½ hours. Arrange pear halves on serving plates. Spoon pineapple mixture evenly over pear halves. Top with granola. Garnish with mint.

Makes 4 servings

Nutrition Information: Serving Size about 1 cup, Calories 150, Total Fat 2g, Saturated Fat 0g, Protein 1g, Carbohydrate 35g, Cholesterol 0mg, Dietary Fiber 4g, Sodium 4mg

Apple and Granola Breakfast Cobbler

4 **medium Granny Smith apples, peeled, cored and sliced**

½ **cup packed light brown sugar**

1 **tablespoon lemon juice**

1 **teaspoon ground cinnamon**

2 **cups granola cereal, plus additional for garnish**

2 **tablespoons butter, cubed**

Cream, half-and-half or yogurt (optional)

Place apples in **CROCK-POT®** slow cooker. Sprinkle with brown sugar, lemon juice and cinnamon. Stir in 2 cups granola and butter. Cover; cook on LOW 6 hours or on HIGH 2 to 3 hours. Serve warm; garnished with additional granola and cream.

Makes 4 servings

Nutrition Information: Serving Size about 1 cup, Calories 393, Total Fat 11g, Saturated Fat 4g, Protein 5g, Carbohydrate 73g, Cholesterol 15mg, Dietary Fiber 8g, Sodium 30mg

Chai Tea

8 cups water

8 bags black tea

¾ cup sugar*

2½ teaspoons ground cardamom (optional)

2½ teaspoons ground cinnamon

2 teaspoons ground cloves

8 slices fresh ginger

1 cup reduced-fat (2%) milk

*Chai tea is typically sweet. For less sweet tea, reduce sugar to ½ cup.

1. Combine water, tea bags, sugar, cardamom, if desired, cinnamon, cloves and ginger in **CROCK-POT®** slow cooker. Cover; cook on HIGH 2 to 2½ hours.

2. Strain mixture; discard solids. (At this point, tea may be covered and refrigerated up to three days.)

3. Stir in milk just before serving. Serve warm or chilled.

Makes 10 servings

Nutrition Information: Serving Size 1 scant cup, Calories 77, Total Fat 1g, Saturated Fat 0g, Protein 1g, Carbohydrate 18g, Cholesterol 2mg, Dietary Fiber 1g, Sodium 21mg

Breakfast

Bacon and Cheese Brunch Potatoes

3 **medium russet potatoes (about 2 pounds), unpeeled and cut into 1-inch pieces**

1 **cup chopped onion**

½ **teaspoon seasoned salt**

4 **slices bacon, crisp-cooked and crumbled**

1 **cup (4 ounces) shredded sharp Cheddar cheese**

1 **tablespoon water**

1. Coat inside of **CROCK-POT®** slow cooker with nonstick cooking spray. Place half of potatoes in **CROCK-POT®** slow cooker. Sprinkle ½ cup onion and ¼ teaspoon seasoned salt over potatoes; top with 2 slices bacon and ½ cup cheese. Repeat layers, ending with remaining ½ cup cheese. Sprinkle water over top.

2. Cover; cook on LOW 6 hours or on HIGH 3½ hours or until potatoes and onion are tender. Stir gently to mix.

Makes 6 servings

Nutrition Information: Serving Size about 1 cup, Calories 197, Total Fat 8g, Saturated Fat 4g, Protein 9g, Carbohydrate 22g, Cholesterol 26mg, Dietary Fiber 2g, Sodium 379mg

Cinnamon Latté

6 cups double-strength brewed coffee*

2 cups half-and-half

1 cup sugar

1 teaspoon vanilla

1½ teaspoons ground cinnamon

Whipped cream (optional)

Cinnamon sticks (optional)

*Double the amount of coffee grounds normally used to brew coffee. Or substitute 8 teaspoons instant coffee dissolved in 6 cups boiling water.

Blend coffee, half-and-half, sugar and vanilla in 3- to 4-quart **CROCK-POT®** slow cooker. Add ground cinnamon. Cover; cook on HIGH 3 hours. Serve in tall coffee mugs. Garnish with whipped cream and cinnamon sticks.

Makes 8 servings

Nutrition Information: Serving Size 1 cup, Calories 180, Total Fat 7g, Saturated Fat 4g, Protein 2g, Carbohydrate 28g, Cholesterol 22mg, Dietary Fiber 0g, Sodium 29mg

Chilies, Soups & Stews

Black Bean and Turkey Stew

3 **cans (about 15 ounces *each*) reduced-sodium black beans, rinsed and drained**

1½ **cups chopped yellow onions**

1½ **cups fat-free reduced-sodium chicken broth**

1 **cup sliced celery**

1 **cup chopped red bell pepper**

4 **cloves garlic, minced**

1½ **teaspoons dried oregano**

¾ **teaspoon ground coriander**

½ **teaspoon ground cumin**

¼ **teaspoon ground red pepper**

6 **ounces cooked turkey sausage, thinly sliced**

1. Combine beans, onions, broth, celery, bell pepper, garlic, oregano, coriander, cumin and ground red pepper in **CROCK-POT®** slow cooker. Cover; cook on LOW 6 to 8 hours.

2. Remove about 1½ cups bean mixture from **CROCK-POT®** slow cooker to blender or food processor; purée bean mixture. Return to **CROCK-POT®** slow cooker. Stir in sausage. Cover; cook on LOW 10 to 15 minutes.

Makes 6 servings

Nutrition Information: Serving Size about 1½ cups, Calories 193, Total Fat 3g, Saturated Fat 1g, Protein 15g, Carbohydrate 35g, Cholesterol 21mg, Dietary Fiber 12g, Sodium 732mg

Chinese Chicken Stew

- **1 pound boneless, skinless chicken thighs, cut into 1-inch pieces**
- **1 teaspoon Chinese five-spice powder***
- **½ teaspoon red pepper flakes**
- **1 tablespoon vegetable oil**
- **1 large yellow onion, coarsely chopped**
- **1 package (8 ounces) mushrooms, sliced**
- **2 cloves garlic, minced**
- **1 can (about 14 ounces) 99% fat-free chicken broth, divided**
- **1 tablespoon cornstarch**
- **1 large red bell pepper, cut into ¾-inch pieces**
- **2 tablespoons soy sauce**
- **2 large green onions, cut into ½-inch pieces**
- **1 tablespoon sesame oil**
- **3 cups hot cooked rice (optional)**
- **¼ cup coarsely chopped fresh cilantro (optional)**

*Chinese five-spice powder is a blend of cinnamon, cloves, fennel seed, anise and Szechuan peppercorns. It is available in most supermarkets and at Asian grocery stores.

1. Toss chicken with five-spice powder and red pepper flakes in large bowl. Heat vegetable oil in large skillet over medium-high heat. Add chicken and onion; cook and stir 5 minutes or until chicken is browned. Add mushrooms and garlic; cook and stir until chicken is no longer pink.

2. Stir ¼ cup broth into cornstarch in small bowl until smooth; set aside. Place cooked chicken mixture, remaining broth, bell pepper and soy sauce in **CROCK-POT®** slow cooker. Cover; cook on LOW 3½ hours.

3. Whisk in cornstarch mixture, green onions and sesame oil. Cover; cook on LOW 30 to 45 minutes or until thickened. Serve with rice, if desired. Garnish with cilantro.

Makes 6 servings

Nutrition Information: Serving Size about 1 cup, Calories 172, Total Fat 10g, Saturated Fat 3g, Protein 17g, Carbohydrate 9g, Cholesterol 61mg, Dietary Fiber 1g, Sodium 759mg

Chilies, Soups & Stews

Asian Beef Stew

1½ **pounds round steak, thinly sliced**

2 **medium yellow onions, cut into ¼-inch slices**

2 **stalks celery, sliced**

2 **carrots, sliced or 1 cup baby carrots**

1 **cup sliced mushrooms**

1 **cup orange juice**

1 **cup beef broth**

⅓ **cup hoisin sauce**

2 **tablespoons cornstarch**

1 **to 2 teaspoons Chinese five-spice powder or curry powder***

1 **cup frozen peas, thawed**

Hot cooked rice (optional)

Chopped fresh cilantro (optional)

*Chinese five-spice powder is a blend of cinnamon, cloves, fennel seed, anise and Szechuan peppercorns. It is available in most supermarkets and at Asian grocery stores.

1. Place beef, onions, celery, carrots and mushrooms in **CROCK-POT®** slow cooker.

2. Combine orange juice, broth, hoisin sauce, cornstarch and five-spice powder in small bowl; pour into **CROCK-POT®** slow cooker. Cover; cook on LOW 6 to 8 hours or on HIGH 5 hours.

3. Stir in peas. Cover; cook on LOW 20 minutes or until peas are tender. Serve with rice, if desired. Garnish with cilantro.

Makes 6 servings

Nutrition Information: Serving Size 1½ cups, Calories 415, Total Fat 5g, Saturated Fat 2g, Protein 30g, Carbohydrate 59g, Cholesterol 63mg, Dietary Fiber 3g, Sodium 423mg

Parsnip and Carrot Soup

Nonstick cooking spray

1 **medium leek, thinly sliced**

4 **medium parsnips, diced**

4 **medium carrots, diced**

4 **cups 99% fat-free reduced-sodium chicken broth**

1 **whole bay leaf**

¼ **teaspoon salt**

½ **teaspoon black pepper**

2 **ounces small pasta, cooked and drained**

1 **tablespoon chopped fresh Italian parsley**

1 **cup fat-free croutons (optional)**

Note

This dish is a great year-round accompaniment to a main course of roasted meat. Or, the soup can stand alone as a quick, satisfying meal all on its own.

1. Spray small skillet with cooking spray; heat over medium heat. Add leek; cook until golden. Remove to **CROCK-POT®** slow cooker.

2. Add parsnips, carrots, broth, bay leaf, salt and pepper. Cover; cook on LOW 6 to 9 hours or on HIGH 2 to 4 hours. Add pasta during last hour of cooking.

3. Remove and discard bay leaf. Sprinkle each serving evenly with parsley and croutons, if desired.

Makes 4 servings

Nutrition Information: Serving Size about 1½ cups, Calories 196, Total Fat 1g, Saturated Fat 0g, Protein 5g, Carbohydrate 44g, Cholesterol 0mg, Dietary Fiber 9g, Sodium 800mg

Beef Chuck Chili

¼ **cup olive oil, divided**

3 **pounds lean beef chuck roast, trimmed***

3 **cups minced yellow onions**

4 **poblano peppers, seeded and diced****

2 **serrano peppers, seeded and diced****

2 **green bell peppers, diced**

3 **jalapeño peppers, seeded and diced****

2 **tablespoons minced garlic**

1 **can (about 28 ounces) crushed tomatoes**

4 **ounces Mexican lager beer (optional)**

¼ **cup hot pepper sauce**

1 **tablespoon ground cumin**

Black pepper (optional)

Corn bread or hot cooked rice (optional)

*Unless you have a 5-, 6- or 7-quart CROCK-POT® slow cooker, cut any roast larger than 2½ pounds in half so it cooks completely.

**Poblano, serrano and jalapeño peppers can sting and irritate the skin, so wear rubber gloves when handling peppers and do not touch your eyes.

1. Heat 2 tablespoons oil in large skillet over medium-high heat. Add chuck roast; brown on both sides. Remove to **CROCK-POT®** slow cooker.

2. Heat remaining 2 tablespoons oil in same skillet over low heat. Add onions, poblano peppers, serrano peppers, bell peppers, jalapeño peppers and garlic; cook and stir 7 minutes or until onions are tender. Remove to **CROCK-POT®** slow cooker. Add tomatoes. Cover; cook on LOW 4 to 5 hours or until beef is fork-tender.

3. Remove beef to cutting board. Shred beef with two forks. Add beer, if desired, hot pepper sauce and cumin to cooking liquid. Season with black pepper, if desired. Return beef to cooking liquid; mix well. Serve over corn bread, if desired.

Makes 10 servings

Nutrition Information: Serving Size about 1 cup, Calories 298, Total Fat 12g, Saturated Fat 3g, Protein 32g, Carbohydrate 14g, Cholesterol 60mg, Dietary Fiber 3g, Sodium 360mg

Creamy Cauliflower Bisque

2 **cans (about 14 ounces *each*) fat-free reduced-sodium chicken broth**

1 **pound frozen cauliflower florets**

1 **pound baking potatoes, cut into 1-inch cubes**

1 **cup chopped yellow onion**

½ **teaspoon dried thyme**

¼ **teaspoon garlic powder**

⅛ **teaspoon ground red pepper**

1 **cup fat-free evaporated milk**

2 **tablespoons unsalted butter**

½ **teaspoon salt**

¼ **teaspoon black pepper**

1 **cup (4 ounces) shredded reduced-fat sharp Cheddar cheese**

¼ **cup finely chopped fresh Italian parsley**

¼ **cup finely chopped green onions**

1. Combine broth, cauliflower, potatoes, onion, thyme, garlic powder and ground red pepper in **CROCK-POT®** slow cooker. Cover; cook on LOW 8 hours or on HIGH 4 hours.

2. Pour soup in batches into food processor or blender; process until smooth. Return to **CROCK-POT®** slow cooker. Add evaporated milk, butter, salt and black pepper; stir until blended. Top servings evenly with cheese, parsley and green onions.

Makes 9 servings

Nutrition Information: Serving Size about 1¼ cups, Calories 142, Total Fat 6g, Saturated Fat 3g, Protein 8g, Carbohydrate 17g, Cholesterol 17mg, Dietary Fiber 2g, Sodium 473mg

Chicken Tortilla Soup

1 **pound boneless, skinless chicken breasts**

2 **cans (15 ounces** *each***) diced tomatoes**

1 **can (4 ounces) chopped mild green chiles, drained**

½ **cup 99% fat-free chicken broth**

1 **medium yellow onion, diced**

2 **cloves garlic, minced**

1 **teaspoon ground cumin**

Salt and black pepper (optional)

4 **corn tortillas, sliced into ¼-inch strips**

2 **tablespoons chopped fresh cilantro**

½ **cup (2 ounces) shredded Monterey Jack cheese**

1 **avocado, peeled, diced and tossed with lime juice**

1. Place chicken in **CROCK-POT**® slow cooker. Combine tomatoes, chiles, broth, onion, garlic and cumin in medium bowl; pour over chicken. Cover; cook on LOW 6 hours or on HIGH 3 hours or until chicken is cooked through.

2. Remove chicken to cutting board. Shred with two forks; return to cooking liquid. Season with salt and pepper, if desired.

3. Just before serving, add tortillas and cilantro to **CROCK-POT**® slow cooker; stir to blend. Serve in soup bowls, topping each serving evenly with cheese and avocado.

Makes 6 servings

Nutrition Information: Serving Size about 1¼ cups, Calories 254, Total Fat 10g, Saturated Fat 3g, Protein 22g, Carbohydrate 19g, Cholesterol 57mg, Dietary Fiber 5g, Sodium 573mg

Smoked Sausage and Bean Soup

2	cans (about 14 ounces *each*) 99% fat-free chicken broth
1½	cups hot water
1	cup dried black beans, rinsed and sorted
1	cup chopped yellow onion
2	whole bay leaves
1	teaspoon sugar
⅛	teaspoon ground red pepper
	Nonstick cooking spray
6	ounces reduced-fat smoked sausage
1	cup chopped tomato
1	tablespoon Worcestershire sauce
2	teaspoons extra virgin olive oil
1	tablespoon chili powder
1½	teaspoons ground cumin
½	teaspoon salt
¼	cup chopped fresh cilantro

1. Combine broth, water, beans, onion, bay leaves, sugar and ground red pepper in **CROCK-POT®** slow cooker. Cover; cook on LOW 8 hours or on HIGH 4 hours.

2. Spray large skillet with cooking spray; heat over medium-high heat. Add sausage; cook 6 to 8 minutes or until beginning to brown, stirring to break up meat. Drain fat.

3. Add sausage, tomato, Worcestershire sauce, oil, chili powder, cumin and salt to **CROCK-POT®** slow cooker. Cover; cook on HIGH 15 minutes. Sprinkle with cilantro.

Makes 9 servings

Nutrition Information: Serving Size about 1 cup, Calories 150, Total Fat 5g, Saturated Fat 1g, Protein 9g, Carbohydrate 18g, Cholesterol 12mg, Dietary Fiber 4g, Sodium 703mg

Shrimp and Pepper Bisque

1 **bag (12 ounces) frozen bell pepper stir-fry mix, thawed**

½ **pound frozen cauliflower florets, thawed**

1 **can (about 14 ounces) 99% fat-free reduced-sodium chicken broth**

1 **stalk celery, sliced**

1 **tablespoon seafood seasoning**

½ **teaspoon dried thyme**

12 **ounces medium raw shrimp, peeled**

2 **cups fat-free half-and-half**

2 **green onions, finely chopped**

Tip
For a creamier, smoother consistency, strain through several layers of damp cheesecloth.

1. Combine stir-fry mix, cauliflower, broth, celery, seafood seasoning and thyme in **CROCK-POT®** slow cooker. Cover; cook on LOW 8 hours or on HIGH 4 hours.

2. Stir in shrimp. Cover; cook on HIGH 15 minutes or until shrimp are pink and opaque. Pour soup in batches into food processor or blender; purée. Return to **CROCK-POT®** slow cooker. Stir in half-and-half. Ladle into cups and sprinkle with green onions.

Makes 4 servings

Nutrition Information: Serving Size about 1 cup, Calories 207, Total Fat 13g, Saturated Fat 1g, Protein 23g, Carbohydrate 19g, Cholesterol 135mg, Dietary Fiber 3g, Sodium 785mg

Thai Coconut Chicken and Rice Soup

1 pound boneless, skinless chicken thighs, cut into **1-inch pieces**

3 cups fat-free reduced-sodium chicken broth

1 package (12 ounces) frozen chopped onions

1 can (4 ounces) sliced mushrooms, drained

2 tablespoons minced fresh ginger

2 tablespoons sugar

1 cup cooked long grain rice

1 can (15 ounces) unsweetened coconut milk

½ red bell pepper, thinly sliced

3 tablespoons chopped fresh cilantro

2 tablespoons grated lime peel

1. Combine chicken, broth, onions, mushrooms, ginger and sugar in **CROCK-POT®** slow cooker. Cover; cook on LOW 8 to 9 hours.

2. Stir rice, coconut milk and bell pepper into soup. Cover; cook on LOW 15 minutes. Turn off heat. Stir in cilantro and lime peel.

Makes 8 servings

Nutrition Information: Serving Size about 1 cup, Calories 158, Total Fat 7g, Saturated Fat 4g, Protein 12g, Carbohydrate 14g, Cholesterol 46mg, Dietary Fiber 1g, Sodium 260mg

Hearty Lentil and Root Vegetable Stew

2 cans (about 14 ounces *each*) 99% fat-free chicken broth

1½ cups turnips, cut into 1-inch pieces

1 cup dried red lentils, rinsed and sorted

1 medium yellow onion, cut into ½-inch wedges

2 medium carrots, cut into 1-inch pieces

1 medium red bell pepper, cut into 1-inch pieces

½ teaspoon dried oregano

⅛ teaspoon red pepper flakes

1 tablespoon olive oil

½ teaspoon salt

4 slices bacon, crisp-cooked and crumbled

½ cup finely chopped green onions

1. Combine broth, turnips, lentils, onion, carrots, bell pepper, oregano and red pepper flakes in **CROCK-POT®** slow cooker; stir to mix well. Cover; cook on LOW 6 hours or on HIGH 3 hours or until lentils are tender.

2. Stir in oil and salt. Sprinkle each serving evenly with bacon and green onions.

Makes 8 servings

Nutrition Information: Serving Size about 1¼ cups, Calories 152, Total Fat 4g, Saturated Fat 1g, Protein 9g, Carbohydrate 20g, Cholesterol 4mg, Dietary Fiber 5g, Sodium 679mg

Curried Butternut Squash Soup

2 pounds butternut squash, rinsed, peeled, cored and chopped into 1-inch cubes

1 firm crisp apple, peeled, cored and chopped

1 medium yellow onion, chopped

5 cups 99% fat-free chicken broth

1 tablespoon curry powder

¼ teaspoon ground cloves

    Salt and black pepper (optional)

¼ cup chopped dried cranberries (optional)

1. Place squash, apple and onion in **CROCK-POT®** slow cooker.

2. Combine broth, curry powder and cloves in small bowl. Pour mixture into **CROCK-POT®** slow cooker. Cover; cook on LOW 5 to 5½ hours or on HIGH 4 hours or until vegetables are tender.

3. Place soup in batches in food processor or blender; process to desired consistency. Season with salt and pepper, if desired. Garnish with cranberries.

Makes 8 servings

Nutrition Information: Serving Size about 1½ cups, Calories 132, Total Fat 1g, Saturated Fat 0g, Protein 4g, Carbohydrate 31g, Cholesterol 0mg, Dietary Fiber 6g, Sodium 592mg

Sweet Potato Stew

1 cup chopped yellow onion

1 cup chopped celery

1 cup grated sweet potato

1 cup reduced-sodium vegetable broth

2 slices bacon, crisp-cooked and crumbled

1 cup fat-free half-and-half

Black pepper (optional)

¼ cup minced fresh parsley

1. Place onion, celery, sweet potato, broth and bacon in **CROCK-POT**® slow cooker. Cover; cook on LOW 6 hours.

2. Turn **CROCK-POT**® slow cooker to HIGH. Stir in half-and-half. Add water, if needed, to reach desired consistency. Cook, uncovered, on HIGH 30 minutes or until heated through. Season with pepper, if desired. Stir in parsley.

Makes 4 servings

Nutrition Information: Serving Size about 1¼ cups, Calories 116, Total Fat 2g, Saturated Fat 1g, Protein 5g, Carbohydrate 18g, Cholesterol 5mg, Dietary Fiber 2g, Sodium 223mg

Chilies, Soups & Stews

Mushroom Barley Stew

1 tablespoon olive oil

1 medium yellow onion, finely chopped

1 cup chopped carrots (about 2 carrots)

1 clove garlic, minced

5 cups reduced-sodium vegetable broth

1 cup uncooked pearl barley

1 cup dried wild mushrooms, broken into pieces

1 teaspoon salt

½ teaspoon dried thyme

½ teaspoon black pepper

Variation

To turn this thick, robust stew into a soup, add 2 to 3 additional cups of broth. Cover; cook on LOW the same amount of time.

1. Heat oil in medium skillet over medium-high heat. Add onion, carrots and garlic; cook and stir 5 minutes or until tender. Place in **CROCK-POT®** slow cooker.

2. Add broth, barley, mushrooms, salt, thyme and pepper to **CROCK-POT®** slow cooker; stir well to combine. Cover; cook on LOW 6 to 7 hours.

Makes 4 servings

Nutrition Information: Serving Size about 1½ cups, Calories 253, Total Fat 4g, Saturated Fat 1g, Protein 10g, Carbohydrate 44g, Cholesterol 0mg, Dietary Fiber 10g, Sodium 530mg

Beef, Lentil and Onion Soup

Nonstick cooking spray

¾ **pound cubed beef stew meat**

2 **cups chopped carrots**

1 **cup sliced celery**

1 **cup dried lentils, rinsed and sorted**

2 **teaspoons dried thyme**

⅛ **teaspoon salt**

¼ **teaspoon black pepper**

3¼ **cups water**

1 **can (10½ ounces) condensed French onion soup, undiluted**

1. Spray large skillet with cooking spray. Heat skillet over medium-high heat. Add beef; cook until browned on all sides.

2. Place carrots, celery and lentils in **CROCK-POT®** slow cooker. Top with beef. Sprinkle with thyme, salt and pepper. Pour water and soup over mixture. Cover; cook on LOW 7 to 8 hours or on HIGH 3½ to 4 hours or until meat and lentils are tender.

Makes 4 servings

Nutrition Information: Serving Size about 1½ cups, Calories 266, Total Fat 10g, Saturated Fat 4g, Protein 24g, Carbohydrate 21g, Cholesterol 57mg, Dietary Fiber 7g, Sodium 740mg

Chilies, Soups & Stews

Black and White Chili

Nonstick cooking spray

1 pound boneless, skinless chicken breasts, cut into ³/₄-inch pieces

1 cup coarsely chopped yellow onion

1 can (about 15 ounces) Great Northern beans, rinsed and drained

1 can (about 15 ounces) reduced-sodium black beans, rinsed and drained

1 can (about 14 ounces) sodium-free stewed tomatoes, undrained

2 tablespoons Texas-style chili seasoning mix

Serving Suggestion

For a change of pace, this delicious chili is excellent served over cooked rice or pasta.

1. Spray large skillet with cooking spray; heat over medium heat. Add chicken and onion; cook and stir 5 minutes or until chicken is browned.

2. Combine chicken mixture, beans, tomatoes and chili seasoning in **CROCK-POT®** slow cooker. Cover; cook on LOW 4 to 4¹/₂ hours.

Makes 6 servings

Nutrition Information: Serving Size about 1¹/₄ cups, Calories 353, Total Fat 12g, Saturated Fat 3g, Protein 20g, Carbohydrate 43g, Cholesterol 31mg, Dietary Fiber 9g, Sodium 681mg

Russian Borscht

4 **cups thinly sliced green cabbage**

1½ **pounds fresh beets, shredded**

5 **small carrots, halved lengthwise then cut into 1-inch pieces**

1 **parsnip, peeled, halved lengthwise then cut into 1-inch pieces**

1 **cup chopped onion**

4 **cloves garlic, minced**

1 **pound cubed beef stew meat**

1 **can (about 14 ounces) diced tomatoes**

3 **cans (about 14 ounces *each*) 99% fat-free reduced-sodium beef broth**

¼ **cup lemon juice**

1 **tablespoon sugar**

1 **teaspoon black pepper**

Sour cream (optional)

Fresh Italian parsley (optional)

Layer cabbage, beets, carrots, parsnip, onion, garlic, beef, tomatoes, broth, lemon juice, sugar and pepper in **CROCK-POT®** slow cooker. Cover; cook on LOW 7 to 9 hours or until vegetables are crisp-tender. Dollop each serving with sour cream and sprinkle with parsley, if desired.

Makes 12 servings

Nutrition Information: Serving Size about 1 cup, Calories 139, Total Fat 4g, Saturated Fat 1g, Protein 11g, Carbohydrate 15g, Cholesterol 24mg, Dietary Fiber 4g, Sodium 345mg

Chicken and Chile Pepper Stew

1 **pound boneless, skinless chicken thighs, cut into ½-inch pieces**

1 **pound small potatoes, cut lengthwise into halves, then crosswise into slices**

1 **cup chopped yellow onion**

2 **poblano peppers, seeded and cut into ½-inch pieces***

1 **jalapeño pepper, seeded and finely chopped***

3 **cloves garlic, minced**

3 **cups fat-free reduced-sodium chicken broth**

1 **can (about 14 ounces) no-salt-added diced tomatoes**

2 **tablespoons chili powder**

1 **teaspoon dried oregano**

*Poblano and jalapeño peppers can sting and irritate the skin, so wear rubber gloves when handling peppers and do not touch your eyes.

1. Place chicken, potatoes, onion, poblano peppers, jalapeño pepper and garlic in **CROCK-POT®** slow cooker.

2. Combine broth, tomatoes, chili powder and oregano in large bowl. Pour into **CROCK-POT®** slow cooker; stir well to blend. Cover; cook on LOW 8 to 9 hours.

Makes 6 servings

Nutrition Information: Serving Size about 1¼ cups, Calories 192, Total Fat 6g, Saturated Fat 2g, Protein 18g, Carbohydrate 22g, Cholesterol 61mg, Dietary Fiber 4g, Sodium 310mg

Chili with Turkey and Beans

2 **cans (about 14 ounces *each*) sodium-free whole tomatoes, drained**

2 **cans (about 15 ounces *each*) sodium-free red kidney beans, rinsed and drained**

1 **pound cooked 99% fat-free ground turkey**

1 **can (about 15 ounces) reduced-sodium black beans, rinsed and drained**

1 **can (12 ounces) sodium-free tomato sauce**

1 **cup finely chopped yellow onion**

1 **cup finely chopped celery**

1 **cup finely chopped carrot**

½ **cup amaretto (optional)**

3 **tablespoons chili powder**

1 **tablespoon Worcestershire sauce**

1 **tablespoon plus 1 teaspoon ground cumin**

2 **teaspoons ground red pepper**

1 **teaspoon salt**

 Shredded Cheddar cheese (optional)

Combine tomatoes, kidney beans, turkey, black beans, tomato sauce, onion, celery, carrot, amaretto, if desired, chili powder, Worcestershire sauce, cumin, ground red pepper and salt in **CROCK-POT®** slow cooker. Cover; cook on HIGH 7 hours. Sprinkle with cheese.

Makes 6 servings

Nutrition Information: Serving Size about 1¼ cups, Calories 301, Total Fat 2g, Saturated Fat 0g, Protein 33g, Carbohydrate 43g, Cholesterol 30mg, Dietary Fiber 18g, Sodium 771mg

Butternut Squash and Apple Soup

3 packages (12 ounces *each*) frozen cooked winter squash, thawed and drained *or* about 4½ cups mashed cooked butternut squash

2 cans (about 14 ounces *each*) 99% fat-free chicken broth

1 medium Golden Delicious apple, peeled, cored and chopped

2 tablespoons minced yellow onion

1 tablespoon packed brown sugar

1 teaspoon minced fresh sage *or* ½ teaspoon ground sage

¼ teaspoon ground ginger

½ cup whipping cream or half-and-half

Tip
For thicker soup, use only 3 cups chicken broth.

Combine squash, broth, apple, onion, brown sugar, sage and ginger in **CROCK-POT®** slow cooker. Cover; cook on LOW 6 hours or on HIGH 3 hours or until squash is tender. Pour soup in food processor or blender; purée. Stir in cream just before serving.

Makes 8 servings

Nutrition Information: Serving Size about 1½ cups, Calories 112, Total Fat 2g, Saturated Fat 1g, Protein 3g, Carbohydrate 25g, Cholesterol 6mg, Dietary Fiber 6g, Sodium 413mg

Vegetarian Chili

1 tablespoon vegetable oil

1 cup chopped yellow onion

1 cup chopped red bell pepper

2 tablespoons minced jalapeño pepper*

1 clove garlic, minced

1 can (28 ounces) sodium-free stewed tomatoes

1 can (about 15 ounces) black beans, rinsed and drained

1 can (about 15 ounces) chickpeas, rinsed and drained

½ cup frozen corn, thawed and drained

¼ cup tomato paste

1 teaspoon sugar

1 teaspoon ground cumin

1 teaspoon dried basil

1 teaspoon chili powder

¼ teaspoon black pepper

Sour cream and shredded Cheddar cheese (optional)

*Jalapeño peppers can sting and irritate the skin, so wear rubber gloves when handling peppers and do not touch your eyes.

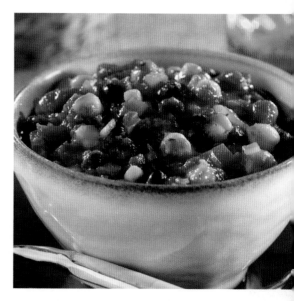

1. Heat oil in large skillet over medium-high heat. Add onion, bell pepper, jalapeño pepper and garlic; cook and stir 5 minutes or until vegetables are tender. Remove vegetables to **CROCK-POT®** slow cooker.

2. Add tomatoes, beans, corn, tomato paste, sugar, cumin, basil, chili powder and black pepper; mix well. Cover; cook on LOW 4 to 5 hours. Serve with sour cream and cheese, if desired.

Makes 4 servings

Nutrition Information: Serving Size about 1½ cups, Calories 329, Total Fat 6g, Saturated Fat 0g, Protein 15g, Carbohydrate 57g, Cholesterol 0mg, Dietary Fiber 14g, Sodium 858mg

Chilies, Soups & Stews

Savory Pea Soup with Sausage

8 ounces smoked sausage, cut lengthwise into halves, then cut into ½-inch pieces

2 cans (about 14 ounces *each*) reduced-sodium chicken broth

1 package (16 ounces) dried split peas, rinsed and sorted

3 medium carrots, sliced

2 stalks celery, sliced

1 medium yellow onion, chopped

¾ teaspoon dried marjoram

1 whole bay leaf

1. Heat medium nonstick skillet over medium heat. Add sausage; cook 5 to 8 minutes or until browned. Drain fat. Combine broth, sausage, peas, carrots, celery, onion, marjoram and bay leaf in **CROCK-POT®** slow cooker.

2. Cover; cook on LOW 4 to 5 hours or until peas are tender. Remove and discard bay leaf. Turn off heat. Cover; let stand 15 minutes to thicken.

Makes 6 servings

Nutrition Information: Serving Size about 1¼ cups, Calories 411, Total Fat 12g, Saturated Fat 4g, Protein 26g, Carbohydrate 52g, Cholesterol 22mg, Dietary Fiber 21g, Sodium 705mg

Lentil and Portobello Soup

2 portobello mushrooms (about 8 ounces total), trimmed

1 tablespoon olive oil

1 medium yellow onion, chopped

2 medium carrots, cut into ½-inch-thick rounds

2 cloves garlic, minced

1 cup dried lentils, rinsed and sorted

1 can (28 ounces) diced tomatoes

1 can (about 14 ounces) vegetable broth

1 teaspoon dried rosemary

1 whole bay leaf

Salt and black pepper (optional)

1. Remove stems from mushrooms; coarsely chop stems. Cut each cap in half, then cut each half into ½-inch pieces.

2. Heat oil in large skillet over medium heat. Add onion, carrots and garlic; cook until onion softens, stirring occasionally. Remove onion mixture to **CROCK-POT®** slow cooker. Layer lentils, tomatoes, broth, mushroom caps and stems, rosemary and bay leaf on top of carrots and onion. Cover; cook on HIGH 5 to 6 hours or until lentils are tender. Remove and discard bay leaf. Season with salt and pepper, if desired. Serve warm.

Makes 6 servings

Nutrition Information: Serving Size about 1½ cups, Calories 185, Total Fat 3g, Saturated Fat 1g, Protein 10g, Carbohydrate 31g, Cholesterol 0mg, Dietary Fiber 11g, Sodium 654mg

Beef Main Dishes

Ginger Beef with Peppers and Mushrooms

- 1½ **pounds beef top round steak, cut into ¾-inch cubes**
- 24 **baby carrots**
- 1 **red bell pepper, chopped**
- 1 **green bell pepper, chopped**
- 1 **medium yellow onion, chopped**
- 1 **package (8 ounces) mushrooms, halved**
- 2 **tablespoons grated fresh ginger**
- 1 **cup 99% fat-free reduced-sodium beef broth**
- ½ **cup hoisin sauce**
- ¼ **cup quick-cooking tapioca**
  Hot cooked rice (optional)

Combine beef, carrots, bell peppers, onion, mushrooms, ginger, broth, hoisin sauce and tapioca in **CROCK-POT®** slow cooker. Cover; cook on LOW 8 to 9 hours. Serve over rice, if desired.

Makes 6 servings

Nutrition Information: Serving Size about 1 cup, Calories 349, Total Fat 11g, Saturated Fat 4g, Protein 38g, Carbohydrate 25g, Cholesterol 66mg, Dietary Fiber 3g, Sodium 502mg

Asian Short Ribs

½ **cup 99% fat-free reduced-sodium beef broth**

¼ **cup reduced-sodium soy sauce**

¼ **cup dry sherry**

1 **tablespoon honey**

1 **tablespoon grated fresh ginger***

2 **teaspoons minced garlic**

2 **pounds boneless beef short ribs**

1 **teaspoon salt**

½ **teaspoon black pepper**

Nonstick cooking spray

Hot cooked rice (optional)

½ **cup chopped green onions (optional)**

*To mince ginger quickly, cut a small piece, remove the skin and put through a garlic press. Store remaining unpeeled ginger in small resealable food storage bag in the refrigerator for up to three weeks.

1. Combine broth, soy sauce, sherry, honey, ginger and garlic in **CROCK-POT®** slow cooker; stir well.

2. Season ribs with salt and pepper. Spray large skillet with cooking spray; heat over medium-high heat. Add beef in batches; cook and stir 6 to 8 minutes or until browned on all sides. Remove to **CROCK-POT®** slow cooker; turn ribs to coat.

3. Cover; cook on LOW 7 to 8 hours or until meat is fork-tender. Remove to serving platter. Serve over rice, if desired. Garnish with green onions.

Makes 6 servings

Nutrition Information: Serving Size about 1¼ cups, Calories 219, Total Fat 12g, Saturated Fat 4g, Protein 22g, Carbohydrate 3g, Cholesterol 67mg, Dietary Fiber 0g, Sodium 660mg

Hearty Beef Short Ribs

1½ pounds flanken-style beef short ribs, bone-in

1 tablespoon black pepper

2¼ teaspoons coarse salt

1 tablespoon olive oil

2 carrots, diced

2 stalks celery, diced

1 large yellow onion, diced

3 cloves garlic, minced

3 whole bay leaves

⅓ cup canned crushed tomatoes

⅓ cup dry red wine

⅓ cup balsamic vinegar

Tip

For a change of pace from ordinary short rib recipes, ask your butcher for flanken-style beef short ribs. Flanken-style ribs are cut across the bones into wide, flat portions. They provide all the meaty flavor of the more common English-style short ribs with smaller, more manageable bones.

1. Season ribs with black pepper and salt. Heat oil in large skillet. Add ribs; cook 2 to 3 minutes on each side or until just browned. Remove to **CROCK-POT®** slow cooker. Add carrots, celery, onion, garlic and bay leaves.

2. Combine tomatoes, wine and vinegar in small bowl. Pour mixture into **CROCK-POT®** slow cooker. Cover; cook on LOW 8 to 9 hours or on HIGH 5½ to 6 hours, turning once or twice, until meat is tender and falling off the bone.

3. Remove ribs from **CROCK-POT®** slow cooker to large serving platter. Pour sauce into food processor or blender; process to desired consistency. To serve, pour sauce evenly over ribs.

Makes 8 servings

Nutrition Information: Serving Size ⅛ ribs and about ¼ cup sauce, Calories 202, Total Fat 11g, Saturated Fat 4g, Protein 17g, Carbohydrate 7g, Cholesterol 50mg, Dietary Fiber 1g, Sodium 632mg

Asian Beef with Mandarin Oranges

  2 **tablespoons vegetable oil**

  2 **pounds lean boneless beef chuck, cut into ½-inch strips**

  1 **small yellow onion, thinly sliced**

  1 **head (about 5 ounces) bok choy, cleaned and chopped**

  1 **can (5 ounces) sliced water chestnuts, drained**

 ⅓ **cup reduced-sodium soy sauce**

  1 **package (about 3 ounces) shiitake mushrooms, sliced**

  1 **small green bell pepper, sliced**

  2 **teaspoons minced fresh ginger**

 ¼ **teaspoon salt**

  1 **can (11 ounces) mandarin oranges in light syrup, drained and syrup reserved**

  2 **tablespoons cornstarch**

  2 **cups 99% fat-free beef broth**

  6 **cups steamed rice**

1. Heat oil in large skillet over medium-high heat. Add beef in batches; cook and stir 6 to 8 minutes or until browned on all sides. Remove to **CROCK-POT®** slow cooker.

2. Add onion to same skillet; cook and stir over medium heat until softened. Add bok choy, water chestnuts, soy sauce, mushrooms, bell pepper, ginger and salt; cook and stir 5 minutes or until bok choy is wilted. Spoon mixture over beef.

3. Stir reserved mandarin orange syrup into cornstarch in medium bowl until smooth. Whisk in broth; pour into **CROCK-POT®** slow cooker. Cover; cook on LOW 10 hours or on HIGH 5 to 6 hours.

4. Stir in mandarin oranges. Spoon 1 cup rice into each serving bowl; spoon ½ cup beef mixture evenly over rice.

Makes 6 servings

Nutrition Information: Serving Size about 1½ cups, Calories 409, Total Fat 12g, Saturated Fat 3g, Protein 29g, Carbohydrate 47g, Cholesterol 65mg, Dietary Fiber 2g, Sodium 717mg

Beef Main Dishes

Braised Chipotle Beef

   3 **pounds lean chuck roast, cut into 2-inch pieces**

   2 **tablespoons vegetable oil, divided**

   1 **large yellow onion, cut into 1-inch pieces**

   2 **red bell peppers, cut into 1-inch pieces**

   3 **tablespoons tomato paste**

   1 **tablespoon chipotle chili powder***

   1 **tablespoon paprika**

   1 **tablespoon ground cumin**

   1 **tablespoon minced garlic**

1½ **teaspoons salt**

   1 **teaspoon dried oregano**

   ½ **teaspoon ground black pepper**

   1 **cup 99% fat-free beef broth**

   1 **can (about 14 ounces) diced tomatoes, drained**

     Hot cooked rice (optional)

You may substitute conventional chili powder.

1. Pat beef dry with paper towels. Heat 1 tablespoon oil in large skillet over medium-high heat. Add beef in batches; cook and stir 6 to 8 minutes or until browned on all sides. Remove to **CROCK-POT**® slow cooker.

2. Return skillet and decrease heat to medium; add remaining 1 tablespoon oil. Add onion; cook and stir until just softened. Add bell peppers; cook 2 minutes. Stir in tomato paste, chili powder, paprika, cumin, garlic, salt, oregano and black pepper; cook and stir 1 minute. Remove to **CROCK-POT**® slow cooker.

3. Return skillet to heat. Add broth, stirring to scrape up any browned bits. Pour over beef in **CROCK-POT**® slow cooker. Stir in tomatoes. Cover; cook on LOW 7 hours. Skim fat from sauce. Serve over rice, if desired.

Makes 8 servings

Nutrition Information: Serving Size about 1 cup, Calories 306, Total Fat 11g, Saturated Fat 3g, Protein 40g, Carbohydrate 9g, Cholesterol 75mg, Dietary Fiber 2g, Sodium 789mg

Meatballs and Spaghetti Sauce

2 pounds 95% lean ground beef

1 cup bread crumbs

1 medium yellow onion, chopped

2 eggs, beaten

¼ cup minced Italian parsley

3 cloves garlic, minced and divided

½ teaspoon dry mustard

½ teaspoon black pepper

3 tablespoons olive oil, divided

1 can (about 28 ounces) whole tomatoes

½ cup chopped fresh basil, plus additional for garnish

1 teaspoon sugar

Hot cooked spaghetti (optional)

1. Combine beef, bread crumbs, onion, eggs, parsley, 1 clove garlic, dry mustard and pepper in large bowl. Form into walnut-sized meatballs. Heat 1 tablespoon oil in large skillet over medium heat. Add meatballs; cook 6 to 8 minutes or until browned on all sides. Remove to **CROCK-POT®** slow cooker.

2. Combine tomatoes, ½ cup basil, remaining 2 tablespoons oil, remaining 2 cloves garlic and sugar in medium bowl. Pour over meatballs, stirring to coat. Cover; cook on LOW 3 to 5 hours or on HIGH 2 to 4 hours. Serve over spaghetti, if desired. Garnish with additional basil.

Makes 8 servings

Nutrition Information: Serving Size about 1 cup, Calories 291, Total Fat 11g, Saturated Fat 4g, Protein 29g, Carbohydrate 16g, Cholesterol 124mg, Dietary Fiber 2g, Sodium 372mg

Beef Main Dishes

Asian Ginger Beef over Bok Choy

2 **tablespoons peanut oil**

1½ **pounds boneless beef chuck roast, cut into 1-inch pieces**

3 **green onions, cut into ½-inch slices**

6 **cloves garlic**

1 **cup 99% fat-free reduced-sodium chicken broth**

½ **cup water**

¼ **cup reduced-sodium soy sauce**

2 **teaspoons ground ginger**

1 **teaspoon Asian chili paste**

9 **ounces fresh udon noodles or vermicelli, cooked and drained**

9 **ounces bok choy, trimmed, washed and cut into 1-inch pieces**

½ **cup minced fresh cilantro**

1. Heat oil in large skillet over medium-high heat. Add beef in batches with green onions and garlic; cook and stir 6 to 8 minutes or until beef is browned on all sides. Remove to **CROCK-POT®** slow cooker. Add broth, water, soy sauce, ginger and chili paste; stir well to combine. Cover; cook on LOW 7 to 8 hours or on HIGH 3 to 4 hours.

2. Stir in noodles and bok choy. Cover; cook on HIGH 15 minutes or until bok choy is tender-crisp. Garnish with cilantro.

Makes 8 servings

Nutrition Information: Serving Size about 1½ cups, Calories 295, Total Fat 10g, Saturated Fat 3g, Protein 24g, Carbohydrate 26g, Cholesterol 49mg, Dietary Fiber 3g, Sodium 488mg

Yankee Pot Roast and Vegetables

- **3** unpeeled medium baking potatoes (about 1 pound), cut into quarters
- **2** large carrots, cut into ¾-inch slices
- **2** stalks celery, cut into ¾-inch slices
- **1** medium yellow onion, sliced
- **1** large parsnip, cut into ¾-inch slices
- **2** whole bay leaves
- **1** teaspoon dried rosemary
- **½** teaspoon dried thyme
- **2½** pounds beef chuck pot roast, cut into 1-inch pieces
  Salt and black pepper (optional)
- **½** cup 99% fat-free reduced-sodium beef broth

Tip

To make gravy, ladle cooking liquid into 2-cup measure; let stand 5 minutes. Skim off fat and discard. Measure remaining cooking liquid and heat to a boil in small saucepan. For each cup of cooking liquid, mix 2 tablespoons all-purpose flour with ¼ cup cold water until smooth. Whisk flour mixture into boiling cooking liquid, stirring constantly 1 minute or until thickened.

1. Combine potatoes, carrots, celery, onion, parsnip, bay leaves, rosemary and thyme in **CROCK-POT**® slow cooker. Season with salt and pepper, if desired. Place beef over vegetables. Pour broth over beef. Cover; cook on LOW 8½ to 9 hours.

2. Remove beef to serving platter; arrange vegetables around beef. Remove and discard bay leaves.

Makes 12 servings

Nutrition Information: Serving Size about 1¼ cups, Calories 182, Total Fat 4g, Saturated Fat 2g, Protein 22g, Carbohydrate 13g, Cholesterol 42mg, Dietary Fiber 3g, Sodium 110mg

Beef Main Dishes

Swiss Steak Stew

- **4 pounds boneless beef top sirloin steaks, each cut into 3 to 4 pieces**
- **2 cans (about 14 ounces *each*) diced tomatoes**
- **2 medium green bell peppers, cut into 1/2-inch strips**
- **2 medium yellow onions, chopped**
- **1 tablespoon seasoned salt**
- **1 teaspoon black pepper**

Add beef, tomatoes, bell peppers, onions, salt and black pepper to **CROCK-POT®** slow cooker. Cover; cook on LOW 8 hours.

Makes 10 servings

Nutrition Information: Serving Size about 1¼ cups, Calories 267, Total Fat 7g, Saturated Fat 3g, Protein 42g, Carbohydrate 7g, Cholesterol 97mg, Dietary Fiber 1g, Sodium 746mg

Easy Beef Stroganoff

- **1½ pounds well-trimmed beef top round steak, cut into 1-inch cubes**
- **4 medium potatoes, cut into 1-inch cubes**
- **4 carrots, cut into 1½-inch pieces *or* 4 cups baby carrots**
- **1 medium yellow onion, cut into 8 wedges**
- **2 cans (8 ounces *each*) tomato sauce**
- **1 teaspoon salt**
- **½ teaspoon black pepper**
- **Hot cooked egg noodles (optional)**
- **Chopped fresh Italian parsley (optional)**

Combine beef, potatoes, carrots, onion, tomato sauce, salt and pepper in **CROCK-POT®** slow cooker. Cover; cook on LOW 8 to 10 hours. Serve over noodles, if desired. Garnish with parsley.

Makes 8 servings

Nutrition Information: Serving Size about 1 cup, Calories 255, Total Fat 9g, Saturated Fat 3g, Protein 20g, Carbohydrate 24g, Cholesterol 54mg, Dietary Fiber 4g, Sodium 681mg

Swiss Steak Stew

Burgundy and Wild Cremini Mushroom Pilaf

- **2 tablespoons vegetable oil**
- **2 cups uncooked converted long grain white rice**
- **1 medium yellow onion, chopped**
- **1 cup sliced wild cremini mushrooms**
- **1 small zucchini, thinly sliced**
- **3¹/₂ cups 99% fat-free beef broth**
- **¹/₂ cup burgundy or other dry red wine**
- **¹/₂ teaspoon salt**
- **¹/₄ teaspoon black pepper**
- **¹/₄ cup (¹/₂ stick) unsalted butter, melted**

1. Heat oil in large skillet over medium heat. Add rice, onion, mushrooms and zucchini; cook and stir 4 to 5 minutes or until rice is slightly browned and onion is tender. Remove to **CROCK-POT®** slow cooker.

2. Add broth, burgundy, salt and pepper. Drizzle melted butter over top; stir once. Cover; cook on LOW 6 to 8 hours.

Makes 6 servings

Nutrition Information: Serving Size about 1¹/₄ cups, Calories 355, Total Fat 11g, Saturated Fat 4g, Protein 6g, Carbohydrate 53g, Cholesterol 15mg, Dietary Fiber 1g, Sodium 720mg

Middle Eastern Beef and Eggplant Stew

1 teaspoon olive oil

1 small eggplant, trimmed and cut into 1-inch pieces

2 cups shiitake or cremini mushrooms, quartered

1 can (about 14 ounces) no-salt-added diced tomatoes

½ pound beef top round steak, cut into 1-inch pieces*

1 medium yellow onion, chopped

1 cup 99% fat-free reduced-sodium beef broth

1 clove garlic, minced

½ teaspoon salt

⅓ teaspoon ground cumin

¼ teaspoon red pepper flakes

¼ teaspoon ground cinnamon

2 teaspoons grated lemon peel

⅛ teaspoon black pepper

***Steak should be trimmed of fat before weighing to yield
½ pound of very lean beef.**

Heat oil in large skillet over medium-high heat. Add eggplant; cook and stir 3 to 5 minutes or until lightly browned on all sides. Remove to **CROCK-POT**® slow cooker. Stir in mushrooms, tomatoes, beef, onion, broth, garlic, salt, cumin, red pepper flakes, cinnamon, lemon peel and black pepper. Cover; cook on LOW 6 hours.

Makes 4 servings

Nutrition Information: Serving Size about 1¼ cups, Calories 183, Total Fat 6g, Saturated Fat 2g, Protein 17g, Carbohydrate 16g, Cholesterol 23mg, Dietary Fiber 6g, Sodium 455mg

Barley Beef Stroganoff

- ⅔ cup uncooked pearl barley
- 2½ cups water
- 1 package (6 ounces) sliced mushrooms
- ½ teaspoon dried marjoram
- ½ pound 95% lean ground beef
- ½ cup chopped celery
- ½ cup minced green onions
- ½ teaspoon black pepper
- ¼ cup fat-free half-and-half
  Minced fresh parsley (optional)

Tip

Browning ground beef before adding it to the **CROCK-POT®** slow cooker helps reduce the fat. Just remember to drain off the fat in the skillet before transferring the meat to the **CROCK-POT®** slow cooker.

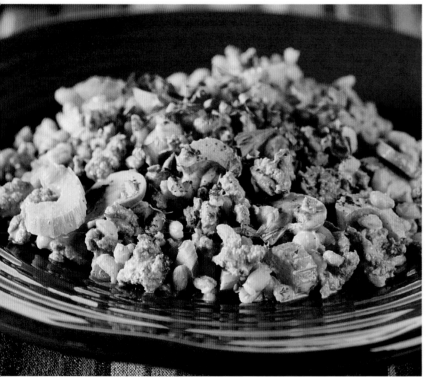

1. Place barley, water, mushrooms and marjoram in **CROCK-POT®** slow cooker. Cover; cook on LOW 6 to 7 hours.

2. Brown beef in large skillet over medium-high heat 6 to 8 minutes, stirring to break up meat. Drain fat. Add celery, green onions and pepper; cook and stir 3 minutes. Remove to **CROCK-POT®** slow cooker.

3. Turn **CROCK-POT®** slow cooker to HIGH. Mix in half-and-half. Cover; cook on HIGH 10 to 15 minutes or until vegetables are tender. Garnish with parsley.

Makes 6 servings

Nutrition Information: Serving Size about 1¼ cups, Calories 160, Total Fat 3g, Saturated Fat 1g, Protein 14g, Carbohydrate 20g, Cholesterol 28mg, Dietary Fiber 4g, Sodium 45mg

Beef Roast with Dark Rum Sauce

1 teaspoon ground allspice

½ teaspoon salt

½ teaspoon black pepper

¼ teaspoon ground cloves

3 pounds lean beef bottom round roast*

2 tablespoons extra virgin olive oil

1 cup dark rum, divided

½ cup 99% fat-free beef broth

2 cloves garlic, minced

2 whole bay leaves, broken in half

½ cup packed dark brown sugar

¼ cup lime juice

***Unless you have a 5-, 6- or 7-quart CROCK-POT® slow cooker, cut any roast larger than 2½ pounds in half so it cooks completely.**

1. Combine allspice, salt, pepper and cloves in small bowl. Rub spices onto all sides of roast.

2. Heat oil in large skillet over medium heat. Add beef; cook 6 to 8 minutes or until browned on all sides. Remove to **CROCK-POT®** slow cooker. Add ½ cup rum, broth, garlic and bay leaves. Cover; cook on LOW 1 hour.

3. Combine remaining ½ cup rum, brown sugar and lime juice in small bowl; stir until well blended. Pour over roast. Cover; cook on LOW 4 to 6 hours, basting beef occasionally with sauce.

4. Remove roast to cutting board; slice. To serve, spoon sauce evenly over beef.

Makes 6 servings

Nutrition Information: Serving Size about 1¼ cups, Calories 467, Total Fat 12g, Saturated Fat 4g, Protein 51g, Carbohydrate 20g, Cholesterol 132mg, Dietary Fiber 0g, Sodium 408mg

Beef Chile Sauce

- **2 tablespoons vegetable oil**
- **2 pounds lean beef round roast, cut into bite-size pieces**
- **1 medium yellow onion, finely chopped**
- **2 cloves garlic, diced**
- **1¾ cups water**
- **5 canned whole mild green chiles, peeled and diced***
- **1 canned chipotle pepper in adobo sauce, diced***
- **1 teaspoon salt**
- **1 teaspoon all-purpose flour**
- **1 teaspoon dried oregano**
- **½ teaspoon ground cumin**
- **¼ teaspoon black pepper**
- **Prepared polenta, cut into ½-inch-thick slices and toasted (optional)**
- **Fresh cilantro (optional)**

*Green chiles and chipotle peppers can sting and irritate the skin, so wear rubber gloves when handling peppers and do not touch your eyes.

1. Heat oil in large skillet over medium heat. Add beef; cook 6 to 8 minutes or until browned on all sides. Add onion and garlic during last few minutes of browning. Remove to **CROCK-POT®** slow cooker.

2. Add water, chiles and chipotle pepper; stir to combine. Cover; cook on LOW 2 hours.

3. Combine salt, flour, oregano, cumin and black pepper in small bowl; stir well to combine. Add to **CROCK-POT®** slow cooker. Cover; cook on LOW 3 to 4 hours. Serve beef mixture over polenta, if desired. Garnish with cilantro.

Makes 6 servings

Nutrition Information: Serving Size about 1¼ cups, Calories 251, Total Fat 11g, Saturated Fat 3g, Protein 34g, Carbohydrate 4g, Cholesterol 88mg, Dietary Fiber 1g, Sodium 527mg

Middle Eastern-Spiced Beef, Tomatoes and Beans

1   **tablespoon extra virgin olive oil**

1½ **pounds lean boneless beef chuck roast, cut into 1-inch pieces and divided**

1   **can (about 14 ounces) no-salt-added diced tomatoes**

1   **cup chopped yellow onion**

6   **ounces fresh green beans, trimmed and broken into 1-inch pieces**

1½ **teaspoons sugar**

½   **teaspoon ground cinnamon**

¼   **teaspoon garlic powder**

¼   **teaspoon ground allspice**

½   **teaspoon salt**

¼   **teaspoon black pepper**

Hot cooked couscous or rice (optional)

1. Heat oil in large skillet over medium-high heat. Add beef in batches; cook and stir 6 to 8 minutes or until browned on all sides. Remove to **CROCK-POT®** slow cooker.

2. Stir in tomatoes, onion, beans, sugar, cinnamon, garlic powder and allspice. Cover; cook on LOW 8 hours or on HIGH 4 hours.

3. Stir in salt and pepper. Turn off heat. Let stand, uncovered, 15 minutes. Serve over couscous, if desired.

Makes about 4 servings

Nutrition Information: Serving Size about 1¼ cups, Calories 326, Total Fat 12g, Saturated Fat 4g, Protein 39g, Carbohydrate 14g, Cholesterol 85mg, Dietary Fiber 3g, Sodium 418mg

Korean Barbecue Beef

- **2 pounds beef short ribs**
- **¼ cup chopped green onions**
- **¼ cup soy sauce**
- **¼ cup water**
- **1 tablespoon packed brown sugar**
- **2 teaspoons minced fresh ginger**
- **2 teaspoons minced garlic**
- **½ teaspoon black pepper**
- **Dark sesame oil (optional)**
- **Hot cooked rice or linguine pasta (optional)**
- **2 teaspoons sesame seeds, toasted (optional)***

*To toast sesame seeds, place in small skillet. Shake skillet over medium-low heat about 3 minutes or until seeds begin to pop and turn golden. Remove from heat.

1. Place ribs in **CROCK-POT®** slow cooker. Combine green onions, soy sauce, water, brown sugar, ginger, garlic and pepper in medium bowl; mix well. Pour over ribs. Cover; cook on LOW 7 to 8 hours or until ribs are fork-tender.

2. Remove ribs to cutting board. Cool slightly. Cut rib meat into bite-size pieces, discarding bones and fat.

3. Turn off heat. Let cooking liquid stand 5 minutes to allow fat to rise. Skim off fat and discard. Stir oil into cooking liquid, if desired. Return beef to **CROCK-POT®** slow cooker. Cover; cook on LOW 15 to 30 minutes or until heated through. Serve over rice, if desired. Garnish with sesame seeds.

Makes 8 servings

Nutrition Information: Serving Size about 1 cup, Calories 214, Total Fat 12g, Saturated Fat 4g, Protein 22g, Carbohydrate 3g, Cholesterol 67mg, Dietary Fiber 0g, Sodium 732mg

Sauvignon Blanc Beef with Beets and Thyme

- **1 pound red or yellow beets, scrubbed and quartered**
- **1 tablespoon extra virgin olive oil**
- **3 pounds lean beef chuck roast***
- **1 medium yellow onion, peeled and quartered**
- **2 cloves garlic, minced**
- **5 sprigs fresh thyme**
- **1 whole bay leaf**
- **2 whole cloves**
- **1 cup 99% fat-free chicken broth**
- **1 cup Sauvignon Blanc or other dry white wine**
- **2 tablespoons tomato paste**
- **Salt and black pepper (optional)**

*Unless you have a 5-, 6- or 7-quart CROCK-POT® slow cooker, cut any roast larger than 2½ pounds in half so it cooks completely.

1. Layer beets evenly in **CROCK-POT®** slow cooker.

2. Heat oil in large skillet over medium heat. Add roast; cook 4 to 5 minutes or until browned on all sides. Add onion and garlic during last few minutes of browning. Remove to **CROCK-POT®** slow cooker. Add thyme, bay leaf and cloves.

3. Combine broth, wine and tomato paste in medium bowl; stir until blended. Season with salt and pepper, if desired. Pour over roast and beets. Cover; cook on LOW 8 to 10 hours or until roast is fork-tender and beets are tender. Remove and discard bay leaf.

Makes 6 servings

Nutrition Information: Serving Size about 1¼ cups, Calories 400, Total Fat 12g, Saturated Fat 4g, Protein 52g, Carbohydrate 11g, Cholesterol 100mg, Dietary Fiber 3g, Sodium 386mg

Beef Main Dishes

Best Beef Brisket Sandwich Ever

     1 **well-trimmed, lean beef brisket (about 3 pounds)**

     2 **cups apple cider, divided**

     1 **head garlic, cloves separated and crushed**

     2 **tablespoons whole peppercorns**

  1/3 **cup chopped fresh thyme or 2 tablespoons dried thyme**

     1 **tablespoon mustard seeds**

     1 **tablespoon Cajun seasoning**

     1 **teaspoon ground allspice**

     1 **teaspoon ground cumin**

     1 **teaspoon celery seeds**

     2 **to 4 whole cloves**

     1 **can (12 ounces) dark beer**

   12 **sourdough sandwich rolls, sliced in half**

*Unless you have a 5-, 6- or 7-quart CROCK-POT® slow cooker, cut any roast larger than 2½ pounds in half so it cooks completely.

1. Place brisket, ½ cup cider, garlic, peppercorns, thyme, mustard seeds, Cajun seasoning, allspice, cumin, celery seeds and cloves in large resealable food storage bag. Seal bag; marinate in refrigerator overnight.

2. Place brisket and marinade in **CROCK-POT®** slow cooker. Add remaining 1½ cups apple cider and beer. Cover; cook on LOW 10 hours or until brisket is tender.

3. Strain sauce; drizzle over meat. Slice brisket and place on sandwich rolls.

Makes 12 servings

Nutrition Information: Serving Size 1 sandwich, Calories 331, Total Fat 5g, Saturated Fat 2g, Protein 30g, Carbohydrate 36g, Cholesterol 46mg, Dietary Fiber 2g, Sodium 558mg

Beef Bourguignonne

- **¹⁄₂ cup all-purpose flour**
- **3 pounds boneless beef top sirloin steak, trimmed of fat and cut into 1-inch pieces**
- **4 slices bacon, diced**
- **2 medium carrots, diced**
- **8 small red potatoes, unpeeled, cut into quarters**
- **8 mushrooms, sliced**
- **20 pearl onions**
- **2¹⁄₂ cups reduced-sodium beef broth**
- **3 cloves garlic, minced**
- **1 whole bay leaf**
- **1 teaspoon dried marjoram**
- **¹⁄₂ teaspoon dried thyme**
- **¹⁄₂ teaspoon salt**
- **Black pepper (optional)**

1. Place flour in large bowl. Add beef; toss to coat. Heat large skillet over medium heat. Add beef and bacon; cook and stir 6 to 8 minutes or until beef is browned on all sides and bacon is crisp. Drain fat.

2. Add carrots, potatoes, mushrooms, onions, broth, garlic, bay leaf, marjoram, thyme, salt, pepper, if desired, and beef mixture to **CROCK-POT®** slow cooker. Cover; cook on LOW 8 to 9 hours. Remove and discard bay leaf.

Makes 10 servings

Nutrition Information: Serving Size about 1¹⁄₄ cups, Calories 367, Total Fat 10g, Saturated Fat 4g, Protein 36g, Carbohydrate 32g, Cholesterol 80mg, Dietary Fiber 3g, Sodium 483mg

Beef Main Dishes

Beef with Green Chiles

- ¼ **cup plus 1 tablespoon all-purpose flour, divided**
- ½ **teaspoon salt**
- ¼ **teaspoon black pepper**
- 1 **pound cubed beef stew meat**
- 1 **tablespoon vegetable oil**
- 2 **cloves garlic, minced**
- 1 **cup 99% fat-free reduced-sodium beef broth**
- 1 **can (7 ounces) diced mild green chiles, drained**
- ½ **teaspoon dried oregano**
- 2 **tablespoons water**
  - **Hot cooked rice (optional)**
  - **Diced tomato (optional)**

Tip
Use 2 cans of chiles for a slightly hotter taste.

1. Combine ¼ cup flour, salt and pepper in large resealable food storage bag. Add beef; shake to coat. Heat oil in large skillet over medium-high heat. Add beef and garlic; cook and stir 6 to 8 minutes or until beef is browned on all sides. Remove beef mixture to **CROCK-POT®** slow cooker. Add broth to skillet, scraping up any browned bits. Pour broth mixture into **CROCK-POT®** slow cooker. Add green chiles and oregano.

2. Cover; cook on LOW 7 to 8 hours. Turn **CROCK-POT®** slow cooker to HIGH. Stir water into remaining 1 tablespoon flour in small bowl until smooth. Whisk into **CROCK-POT®** slow cooker. Cover; cook on HIGH 15 minutes or until thickened. Serve with rice, if desired. Garnish with tomato.

Makes 4 servings

Nutrition Information: Serving Size about 1¼ cups, Calories 234, Total Fat 8g, Saturated Fat 2g, Protein 27g, Carbohydrate 11g, Cholesterol 50mg, Dietary Fiber 2g, Sodium 777mg

Italian-Style Pot Roast

- **2 teaspoons minced garlic**
- **1 teaspoon salt**
- **1 teaspoon dried basil**
- **1 teaspoon dried oregano**
- **¼ teaspoon red pepper flakes**
- **2½ pounds lean boneless beef bottom round rump roast, cut in half**
- **1 large yellow onion, quartered and thinly sliced**
- **1½ cups pasta sauce**
- **2 cans (about 15 ounces *each*) Great Northern beans, rinsed and drained**
- **¼ cup shredded fresh basil**

1. Combine garlic, salt, dried basil, oregano and red pepper flakes in small bowl. Season roast halves with garlic mixture.

2. Place half of onion in **CROCK-POT®** slow cooker. Place one half of roast over onion slices; top with remaining onion slices and other half of roast. Pour pasta sauce over roast. Cover; cook on LOW 8 to 9 hours.

3. Remove roast to cutting board. Cover loosely with foil; let stand 10 to 15 minutes before slicing. Turn off heat. Let liquid in **CROCK-POT®** slow cooker stand 5 minutes; skim off fat.

4. Turn **CROCK-POT®** slow cooker to HIGH. Stir beans into liquid. Cover; cook on HIGH 15 to 30 minutes or until beans are heated through. Serve with bean mixture and fresh basil.

Makes 8 servings

Nutrition Information: Serving Size about 1¼ cups, Calories 372, Total Fat 9g, Saturated Fat 3g, Protein 41g, Carbohydrate 29g, Cholesterol 84mg, Dietary Fiber 6g, Sodium 689mg

Peppered Brisket and Cabbage

12 small new potatoes, quartered

4 carrots, sliced

1 beef brisket (about 2 pounds)

1 head cabbage, cut into wedges

2 medium yellow onions, sliced

3 whole bay leaves

8 whole black peppercorns

¹/₂ teaspoon pickling spice

1. Place potatoes and carrots in bottom of **CROCK-POT®** slow cooker. Add beef, cabbage, onions, bay leaves, peppercorns, pickling spice and enough water to cover brisket. Cover; cook on LOW 4 to 5 hours or on HIGH 2 to 2¹/₂ hours.

2. Remove beef to cutting board. Cover loosely with foil; let stand 10 to 15 minutes before slicing. Remove and discard bay leaves. Serve with vegetables.

Makes 10 servings

Nutrition Information: Serving Size about 1¹/₂ cups, Calories 329, Total Fat 7g, Saturated Fat 2g, Protein 24g, Carbohydrate 42g, Cholesterol 56mg, Dietary Fiber 7g, Sodium 352mg

Italian Braised Short Ribs in Red Wine

3 pounds beef short ribs, trimmed

Salt and black pepper (optional)

2 large yellow onions, sliced

2 cloves garlic, minced

2 packages (8 ounces *each*) baby bella or cremini mushrooms, quartered

2 cups dry red wine

2 cups 99% fat-free beef broth

2 teaspoons Italian seasoning

Mashed potatoes (optional)

1. Coat inside of **CROCK-POT**® slow cooker with nonstick cooking spray. Season ribs with salt and pepper, if desired. Heat large skillet over medium-high heat. Add ribs in batches; cook and stir 6 to 8 minutes or until browned on all sides. Remove to **CROCK-POT**® slow cooker.

2. Return skillet to heat. Add onions; cook and stir 3 to 5 minutes or until tender. Add garlic, mushrooms, wine, broth and Italian seasoning; cook and stir 3 minutes. Pour over ribs. Cover; cook on LOW 10 to 12 hours or on HIGH 6 to 8 hours. Remove ribs and mushrooms to large serving platter. Strain cooking liquid. Serve with mashed potatoes, if desired, and cooking liquid.

Makes 8 servings

Nutrition Information: Serving Size about 1 rib and $1/2$ cup sauce, Calories 279, Total Fat 12g, Saturated Fat 4g, Protein 24g, Carbohydrate 8g, Cholesterol 67mg, Dietary Fiber 1g, Sodium 303mg

Pork Main Dishes

Sauerkraut Pork Ribs

Nonstick cooking spray

2 **pounds country-style pork ribs, trimmed and cut into individual portions**

1 **medium yellow onion, thinly sliced**

1 **teaspoon caraway seeds**

½ **teaspoon garlic powder**

¼ **teaspoon black pepper**

1 **package (about 14 ounces) fresh coleslaw mix**

¾ **cup water**

1 **can (about 14 ounces) sauerkraut**

12 **medium red potatoes, quartered**

1. Spray large skillet with cooking spray; heat over medium-low heat. Add ribs; cook 6 to 8 minutes or until browned on all sides. Remove to **CROCK-POT®** slow cooker.

2. Drain drippings from skillet; discard. Add onion; cook 3 to 5 minutes or until tender. Add caraway seeds, garlic powder and pepper; cook 15 minutes. Remove onion mixture to **CROCK-POT®** slow cooker. Top with coleslaw mix.

3. Add water to skillet, stirring to scrape up any brown bits. Pour skillet juices into **CROCK-POT®** slow cooker. Drain half of canning liquid from sauerkraut; discard. Pour sauerkraut and remaining liquid over meat. Top with potatoes. Cover; cook on LOW 6 to 8 hours or until potatoes are tender, stirring halfway through cooking time.

Makes 6 servings

Nutrition Information: Serving Size ⅙ ribs and ¾ cup vegetable mixture, Calories 496, Total Fat 9g, Saturated Fat 2g, Protein 40g, Carbohydrate 63g, Cholesterol 112mg, Dietary Fiber 9g, Sodium 339mg

Pork Loin Stuffed with Stone Fruits

1 boneless pork loin roast (about 4 pounds)*

¾ teaspoon salt

½ teaspoon black pepper

2 tablespoons olive oil, divided

1 medium yellow onion, chopped

½ cup Madeira or dry sherry wine

½ cup dried pitted plums

½ cup dried peaches

½ cup dried apricots

2 cloves garlic, minced

¼ teaspoon dried thyme

Unless you have a 5-, 6- or 7-quart CROCK-POT® slow cooker, cut any roast larger than 2½ pounds in half so it cooks completely.

Tip

To butterfly a roast means to split the meat down the center without cutting all the way through. This allows the meat to be spread open and a filling can be added.

1. Coat inside of **CROCK-POT®** slow cooker with nonstick cooking spray. Season pork with salt and pepper. Heat 1 tablespoon oil in large skillet over medium-high heat. Add pork; cook 6 to 8 minutes or until browned on all sides. Remove pork to cutting board, browned side down.

2. Add remaining 1 tablespoon oil to same skillet; heat over medium heat. Add onion; cook and stir 3 to 5 minutes or until tender. Add Madeira; cook 2 to 3 minutes or until mixture reduces slightly. Stir in dried fruit, garlic and thyme; cook 1 minute. Remove skillet from heat.

3. Butterfly roast lengthwise to within 1½ inches of edge. Spoon fruit mixture onto pork roast; bring sides together to close roast. Slide kitchen string under roast and tie roast shut, allowing 2 inches between ties. Place roast in **CROCK-POT®** slow cooker. Cover; cook on LOW 5 to 6 hours or on HIGH 2 to 3 hours or until roast is tender.

4. Remove roast to cutting board. Cover loosely with foil; let stand 10 to 15 minutes before slicing. Serve roast with cooking liquid.

Makes 10 servings

Nutrition Information: Serving Size ¹⁄₁₀ roast and about ¾ cup fruit and sauce, Calories 319, Total Fat 11g, Saturated Fat 3g, Protein 39g, Carbohydrate 14g, Cholesterol 114mg, Dietary Fiber 2g, Sodium 270mg

Pork Main Dishes

Pecan and Apple Stuffed Pork Chops with Apple Brandy

- **4 thick-cut, bone-in pork loin chops (about 12 ounces *each*)**
- **1 teaspoon salt, divided**
- **½ teaspoon black pepper, divided**
- **2 tablespoons vegetable oil**
- **½ cup diced green apple**
- **½ small yellow onion, minced**
- **¼ teaspoon dried thyme**
- **½ cup apple brandy or brandy**
- **⅔ cup cubed white bread**
- **1 tablespoon chopped pecans**
- **1 cup apple juice**

1. Coat inside of **CROCK-POT®** slow cooker with nonstick cooking spray. Season pork with ½ teaspoon salt and ¼ teaspoon pepper. Heat oil in large skillet over medium-high heat. Add pork in batches; cook 2 minutes on each side or until browned. Remove from skillet; set aside.

2. Return skillet to medium heat. Add apple, onion, thyme, remaining ½ teaspoon salt and remaining ¼ teaspoon pepper; cook and stir 3 minutes or until onion is tender. Remove from heat. Pour in brandy. Heat over medium heat; simmer until most liquid is absorbed. Stir in bread and pecans; cook 1 minute.

3. Cut each pork chop horizontally with sharp knife to form pocket. Divide stuffing among pork chops. Arrange pork chops in **CROCK-POT®** slow cooker, pocket side up. Pour apple juice around pork chops. Cover; cook on HIGH 1½ to 1¾ hours or until pork is cooked through.

Makes 4 servings

Nutrition Information: Serving Size 1 pork chop and about ⅓ cup stuffing, Calories 415, Total Fat 11g, Saturated Fat 3g, Protein 42g, Carbohydrate 13g, Cholesterol 122mg, Dietary Fiber 1g, Sodium 720mg

Rigatoni with Broccoli Rabe and Sausage

2 tablespoons olive oil

3 sweet or hot Italian sausage links, casings removed

2 cloves garlic, minced

1 large bunch (about 1¼ pounds) broccoli rabe

½ cup 99% fat-free chicken broth or water

½ teaspoon salt

½ teaspoon red pepper flakes

1 pound uncooked rigatoni

Grated Parmesan cheese (optional)

1. Coat inside of **CROCK-POT®** slow cooker with nonstick cooking spray. Heat oil in large skillet over medium heat. Add sausage; cook and stir 6 to 8 minutes, stirring to break up meat. Drain fat. Add garlic; cook and stir 1 minute or until softened and fragrant. Remove to **CROCK-POT®** slow cooker.

2. Trim any stiff, woody parts from bottoms of broccoli rabe stems; discard. Cut broccoli rabe into 1-inch lengths. Place in large bowl of cold water; stir with hands to wash well. Lift broccoli rabe out of water by handfuls leaving any sand or dirt in bottom of bowl. Shake well to remove excess water, but do not dry. Add to **CROCK-POT®** slow cooker with sausage. Add broth, salt and red pepper flakes. Cover; cook on LOW 4 hours or on HIGH 2 hours.

3. Meanwhile, cook rigatoni according to package directions. Stir into sausage mixture just before serving. Garnish with cheese.

Makes 6 servings

Nutrition Information: Serving Size about 1½ cups, Calories 414, Total Fat 10g, Saturated Fat 3g, Protein 21g, Carbohydrate 62g, Cholesterol 13mg, Dietary Fiber 2g, Sodium 545mg

Golden Harvest Pork Stew

  2 tablespoons all-purpose flour, divided

  1 pound boneless pork loin rib roast, cut into 1-inch pieces

  1 tablespoon vegetable oil

  2 medium Yukon Gold potatoes, unpeeled and cut into 1-inch pieces

  1 large sweet potato, peeled and cut into 1-inch pieces

  1 cup chopped carrots

  1 ear corn, broken into 4 pieces *or* ¹/₂ cup corn

¹/₂ cup 99% fat-free reduced-sodium chicken broth

  1 jalapeño pepper, seeded and finely chopped*

  1 clove garlic, minced

  1 teaspoon salt

¹/₄ teaspoon black pepper

¹/₄ teaspoon dried thyme

  Chopped fresh Italian parsley (optional)

*Jalapeño peppers can sting and irritate the skin, so wear rubber gloves when handling peppers and do not touch your eyes.

1. Place 1 tablespoon flour in large resealable food storage bag. Add pork; shake to coat. Heat oil in large skillet over medium-high heat. Add pork; cook and stir 6 to 8 minutes or until browned on all sides. Remove to **CROCK-POT®** slow cooker. Add potatoes, carrots, corn, broth, jalapeño pepper, garlic, salt, black pepper and thyme; stir to blend. Cover; cook on LOW 5 to 6 hours.

2. Turn **CROCK-POT®** slow cooker to HIGH. Stir ¹/₄ cup cooking liquid into remaining 1 tablespoon flour in small bowl until smooth. Whisk into stew. Cover; cook on HIGH 15 minutes or until thickened. Garnish with parsley.

Makes 4 servings

Nutrition Information: Serving Size about 1¹/₂ cups, Calories 329, Total Fat 7g, Saturated Fat 2g, Protein 30g, Carbohydrate 35g, Cholesterol 65mg, Dietary Fiber 5g, Sodium 751mg

Pork Main Dishes

Boneless Pork Roast with Garlic

- **1 lean boneless pork rib roast (2 to 2½ pounds), rinsed and patted dry**
- **Salt and black pepper (optional)**
- **3 tablespoons olive oil, divided**
- **4 cloves garlic, minced**
- **¼ cup chopped fresh rosemary**
- **½ lemon, cut into ⅛- to ¼-inch slices**
- **¼ cup dry white wine (such as Chardonnay)**
- **½ cup 99% fat-free chicken broth**

1. Season pork with salt and pepper, if desired. Combine 2 tablespoons oil, garlic and rosemary in small bowl. Rub over pork. Roll and tie pork snugly with kitchen string. Tuck lemon slices under string and into ends of roast.

2. Heat remaining 1 tablespoon oil in large skillet over medium heat. Add pork; cook 6 to 8 minutes or until browned on all sides. Remove to **CROCK-POT**® slow cooker.

3. Return skillet to heat. Add wine and broth, stirring to scrape up any browned bits. Pour over pork in **CROCK-POT**® slow cooker. Cover; cook on LOW 8 to 9 hours or on HIGH 3½ to 4 hours.

4. Remove pork to cutting board. Cover loosely with foil; let stand 10 to 15 minutes before removing string and slicing. Serve with cooking liquid.

Makes 6 servings

Nutrition Information: Serving Size ⅙ roast, Calories 273, Total Fat 12g, Saturated Fat 3g, Protein 35g, Carbohydrate 2g, Cholesterol 86mg, Dietary Fiber 0g, Sodium 162mg

Pork Main Dishes

Posole

> **3** **pounds boneless pork, cut into 1-inch pieces**
>
> **2** **cans (14 ounces *each*) white hominy, drained**
>
> **1** **package (10 ounces) frozen white corn, thawed**
>
> **¾** **cup chili sauce**
>
> **Sprigs fresh Italian parsley (optional)**

Combine pork, hominy, corn and chili sauce in **CROCK-POT**® slow cooker. Cover; cook on HIGH 5 hours. Turn **CROCK-POT**® slow cooker to LOW. Cover; cook on LOW 10 hours. Garnish with parsley.

Makes 8 servings

Nutrition Information: Serving Size about 1½ cups, Calories 344, Total Fat 6g, Saturated Fat 2g, Protein 42g, Carbohydrate 27g, Cholesterol 97mg, Dietary Fiber 5g, Sodium 646mg

German Kraut and Sausage

> **5** **medium potatoes, cut into ½-inch pieces**
>
> **1** **large yellow onion, cut into ¼-inch slices**
>
> **1** **can (16 ounces) sauerkraut**
>
> **½** **green bell pepper, chopped**
>
> **1** **pound reduced-fat smoked sausage, cut into 1-inch pieces**
>
> **¼** **cup packed brown sugar**
>
> **1** **teaspoon garlic powder**
>
> **½** **teaspoon black pepper**

1. Place potatoes, onion, sauerkraut and bell pepper in **CROCK-POT**® slow cooker.

2. Heat large skillet over medium-high heat. Add sausage; cook and stir 6 to 8 minutes or until browned on all sides. Remove to **CROCK-POT**® slow cooker. Add brown sugar, garlic powder and black pepper. Cover; cook on LOW 8 hours.

Makes 8 servings

Nutrition Information: Serving Size about 1½ cups, Calories 282, Total Fat 11g, Saturated Fat 4g, Protein 13g, Carbohydrate 34g, Cholesterol 41mg, Dietary Fiber 5g, Sodium 550mg

Posole

Pork Main Dishes

Pork Roast with Fruit Medley

1 **boneless pork loin roast (about 4 pounds)***

1 **tablespoon black pepper**

2 **teaspoons salt**

　Nonstick cooking spray

2 **cups green grapes**

1 **cup dried apricots**

1 **cup dried prunes**

2 **whole bay leaves**

1 **teaspoon dried thyme**

2 **cloves garlic, minced**

1 **cup dry red wine**

　Juice of 1/2 lemon

**Unless you have a 5-, 6- or 7-quart CROCK-POT® slow cooker, cut any roast larger than
2 1/2 pounds in half so it cooks completely.*

1. Season pork with pepper and salt. Spray large skillet with cooking spray. Heat over medium-high heat. Add pork; cook 5 to 7 minutes or until browned on all sides.

2. Combine grapes, apricots, prunes, bay leaves, thyme, garlic, wine and lemon juice in **CROCK-POT®** slow cooker; stir to blend. Add pork to **CROCK-POT®** slow cooker; turn to coat. Cover; cook on LOW 7 to 9 hours or on HIGH 3 to 5 hours. Remove and discard bay leaves.

Makes 8 servings

Nutrition Information: Serving Size 1/8 roast and 3/4 cup fruit sauce, Calories 441, Total Fat 10g, Saturated Fat 3g, Protein 49g, Carbohydrate 32g, Cholesterol 142mg, Dietary Fiber 3g, Sodium 776mg

Pork Main Dishes

Ham and Potato Casserole

1½ **pounds red potatoes, unpeeled and sliced**

8 **ounces thinly sliced extra-lean deli ham**

2 **poblano chile peppers, cut into thin slices**

2 **tablespoons olive oil**

1 **tablespoon dried oregano**

¼ **teaspoon salt**

1 **cup (4 ounces) shredded Monterey Jack cheese**

2 **tablespoons finely chopped fresh cilantro**

Combine potatoes, ham, chile peppers, oil, oregano and salt in **CROCK-POT®** slow cooker; stir to blend. Cover; cook on LOW 7 hours or on HIGH 4 hours. Remove potato mixture to large serving platter. Sprinkle with cheese and cilantro; let stand 3 minutes or until cheese is melted.

Makes 6 servings

Nutrition Information: Serving Size ⅙ casserole, Calories 201, Total Fat 10g, Saturated Fat 4g, Protein 12g, Carbohydrate 17g, Cholesterol 32mg, Dietary Fiber 2g, Sodium 543mg

Simply Delicious Pork Roast

1½ **pounds boneless pork loin, cut into 6 pieces *or* 6 boneless pork loin chops**

4 **medium Golden Delicious apples, cored and sliced**

3 **tablespoons packed light brown sugar**

1 **teaspoon ground cinnamon**

½ **teaspoon salt**

Place pork in **CROCK-POT®** slow cooker; cover with apples. Combine brown sugar, cinnamon and salt in small bowl; sprinkle over apples. Cover; cook on LOW 6 to 8 hours.

Makes 6 servings

Nutrition Information: Serving Size ⅙ pork and about 1 cup sauce, Calories 222, Total Fat 4g, Saturated Fat 1g, Protein 26g, Carbohydrate 21g, Cholesterol 65mg, Dietary Fiber 2g, Sodium 259mg

Ham and Potato
Casserole

Pork Main Dishes

Braised Pork Shanks with Israeli Couscous and Root Vegetable Stew

- **4 pork shanks, bone in, skin removed (about 1½ pounds total)**
- **Coarse salt and black pepper (optional)**
- **2 tablespoons olive oil**
- **4 large carrots, sliced diagonally into 1-inch pieces, divided**
- **4 stalks celery, sliced diagonally into 1-inch pieces, divided**
- **1 large yellow onion, quartered**
- **4 cloves garlic, crushed**
- **4 cups fat-free reduced-sodium chicken broth**
- **2 cups dry white wine**
- **¼ cup no-salt-added tomato paste**
- **¼ cup distilled white vinegar**
- **2 tablespoons mustard oil (optional)***
- **1 tablespoon whole black peppercorns**
- **Israeli Couscous (recipe follows)**

*Mustard oil is available in Middle Eastern specialty shops or in the supermarket ethnic foods aisle.

1. Season pork with salt and black pepper, if desired. Heat oil in large skillet over medium heat. Add pork; cook 5 to 7 minutes or until browned on all sides. Remove to **CROCK-POT®** slow cooker.

2. Pour off all but 2 tablespoons oil in skillet. Add half of carrots, half of celery, onion and garlic; cook and stir 5 minutes or until vegetables are soft but not brown. Remove to **CROCK-POT®** slow cooker.

3. Add broth, wine, tomato paste, vinegar, mustard oil, if desired, and peppercorns to skillet; bring to a boil, stirring to scrape up any browned bits. Pour over pork. Cover; cook on HIGH 2 hours, turning pork every 20 minutes.

4. Remove pork. Strain cooking liquid; discard solids. Return cooking liquid to **CROCK-POT®** slow cooker. Add remaining half of carrots and celery; return pork to **CROCK-POT®** slow cooker. Cover; cook on HIGH 1 hour. Remove pork to large plate. Cover loosely with foil to keep warm.

5. Meanwhile, prepare Israeli Couscous.

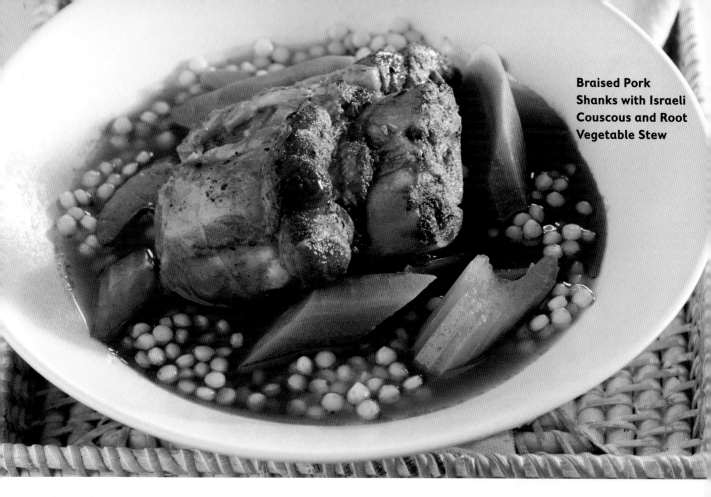

Braised Pork Shanks with Israeli Couscous and Root Vegetable Stew

6. Add Israeli couscous to **CROCK-POT**® slow cooker. Cover; cook on HIGH 5 to 10 minutes or until heated through. Place couscous and vegetables in shallow bowls; top each with 1 pork shank. Spoon ¼ cup cooking liquid into each bowl.

Makes 4 servings

Israeli Couscous

2 cups water

Pinch salt

1⅓ cups Israeli or regular couscous

Place water and salt in large skillet over medium-low heat; bring to a boil over high heat. Add couscous; cook and stir 6 to 8 minutes or until tender. Rinse and drain under cold water.

Nutrition Information: Serving Size 1 pork shank and 1 cup stew, Calories 459, Total Fat 12g, Saturated Fat 3g, Protein 31g, Carbohydrate 44g, Cholesterol 68mg, Dietary Fiber 5g, Sodium 488mg

Italian-Style Sausage with Rice

1 pound mild Italian sausage links, cut into 1-inch pieces

1 can (about 15 ounces) no-salt-added pinto beans, rinsed and drained

1 cup reduced-sodium marinara sauce

1 green bell pepper, cut into strips

1 small yellow onion, halved and sliced

½ teaspoon salt

¼ teaspoon black pepper

Hot cooked rice (optional)

Fresh basil (optional)

1. Brown sausage in large skillet over medium-high heat 6 to 8 minutes. Drain fat.

2. Place sausage, beans, pasta sauce, bell pepper, onion, salt and black pepper in **CROCK-POT®** slow cooker. Cover; cook on LOW 4 to 6 hours or on HIGH 2 to 3 hours. Serve with rice, if desired. Garnish with basil.

Makes 5 servings

Nutrition Information: Serving Size about 1½ cups, Calories 267, Total Fat 8g, Saturated Fat 3g, Protein 19g, Carbohydrate 19g, Cholesterol 27mg, Dietary Fiber 5g, Sodium 800mg

Pork Roast Landaise

2½ **pounds boneless center-cut pork loin roast**

Salt and black pepper (optional)

2 **tablespoons olive oil**

1 **medium yellow onion, diced**

2 **large cloves garlic, minced**

2 **teaspoons dried thyme**

2 **parsnips, cut into ¾-inch slices**

¼ **cup red wine vinegar**

¼ **cup sugar**

½ **cup dry sherry**

2 **cups 99% fat-free chicken broth, divided**

2 **tablespoons cornstarch**

3 **pears, cored and sliced ¾ inch thick**

1½ **cups pitted prunes**

1. Season pork with salt and pepper, if desired. Heat oil in large skillet over medium-high heat. Add pork; cook 5 to 7 minutes on each side or until browned. Remove to **CROCK-POT®** slow cooker.

2. Add onion and garlic to skillet; cook and stir 2 to 3 minutes. Stir in thyme. Remove to **CROCK-POT®** slow cooker. Add parsnips; stir well.

3. Combine vinegar and sugar in same skillet; cook and stir 5 to 7 minutes or until thickened. Add sherry; cook 1 minute. Add 1¾ cups broth. Stir remaining ¼ cup broth into cornstarch in small bowl until smooth. Whisk cornstarch mixture into skillet; cook until slightly thickened. Pour into **CROCK-POT®** slow cooker.

4. Cover; cook on LOW 8 hours or on HIGH 4 hours. Add pears and prunes during last 30 minutes of cooking.

Makes 8 servings

Nutrition Information: Serving Size ⅛ roast and about ½ cup sauce, Calories 407, Total Fat 9g, Saturated Fat 2g, Protein 33g, Carbohydrate 45g, Cholesterol 98mg, Dietary Fiber 5g, Sodium 325mg

Pork Loin with Sherry and Red Onions

1 tablespoon unsalted butter

3 large red onions, thinly sliced

1 cup pearl onions, blanched and peeled

2½ pounds boneless pork loin, tied

½ teaspoon salt

½ teaspoon black pepper

½ cup dry sherry

2 tablespoons chopped fresh Italian parsley

2 tablespoons water

1½ tablespoons cornstarch

Note
The mild flavor of pork is awakened by this rich, delectable sauce.

1. Melt butter in large skillet over medium heat. Add red and pearl onions; cook 3 to 5 minutes or until tender.

2. Season pork with salt and pepper. Place in **CROCK-POT®** slow cooker. Add cooked onions, sherry and parsley. Cover; cook on LOW 8 to 10 hours or on HIGH 5 to 6 hours.

3. Remove pork to cutting board. Cover loosely with foil; let stand 10 to 15 minutes before slicing.

4. Stir water into cornstarch in small bowl until smooth. Whisk into cooking liquid in **CROCK-POT®** slow cooker. Cover; cook on HIGH 15 minutes or until sauce is thickened. Serve pork with onion and sherry sauce.

Makes 8 servings

Nutrition Information: Serving Size ⅛ roast and about ¼ cup sauce, Calories 253, Total Fat 6g, Saturated Fat 3g, Protein 34g, Carbohydrate 13g, Cholesterol 84mg, Dietary Fiber 1g, Sodium 412mg

Mediterranean Meatball Ratatouille

- **1 pound reduced-fat mild Italian sausage**
- **1 package (8 ounces) sliced mushrooms**
- **1 small eggplant, diced**
- **1 zucchini, diced**
- **½ cup chopped yellow onion**
- **1 clove garlic, minced**
- **1 teaspoon dried oregano**
- **1 teaspoon salt**
- **½ teaspoon black pepper**
- **2 fresh tomatoes, diced**
- **1 tablespoon tomato paste**
- **2 tablespoons chopped fresh basil**
- **1 teaspoon lemon juice**

1. Shape sausage into 1-inch meatballs. Heat large skillet over medium heat. Add meatballs; cook and stir 6 to 8 minutes or until browned.

2. Place half of meatballs in **CROCK-POT®** slow cooker. Add half each of mushrooms, eggplant and zucchini. Top with onion, garlic, ½ teaspoon oregano, ½ teaspoon salt and ¼ teaspoon pepper. Add remaining meatballs, mushrooms, eggplant and zucchini, ½ teaspoon oregano, ½ teaspoon salt and ¼ teaspoon pepper. Cover; cook on LOW 6 to 7 hours.

3. Stir in tomatoes and tomato paste. Cover; cook on LOW 15 minutes. Stir in basil and lemon juice just before serving.

Makes 6 servings

Nutrition Information: Serving Size 1⅔ cups, Calories 173, Total Fat 11g, Saturated Fat 4g, Protein 12g, Carbohydrate 9g, Cholesterol 41mg, Dietary Fiber 3g, Sodium 676mg

Panama Pork Stew

2 small sweet potatoes (about ³/₄ pound), cut into 2-inch pieces

1 package (10 ounces) frozen corn, thawed

1 package (9 ounces) frozen cut green beans, thawed

1 cup chopped yellow onion

1¹/₄ pounds boneless pork top loin roast, cut into 1-inch pieces

1 can (about 14 ounces) diced tomatoes

¹/₄ cup water

1 tablespoon chili powder

¹/₂ teaspoon salt

¹/₂ teaspoon ground coriander

Place potatoes, corn, green beans and onion in **CROCK-POT®** slow cooker; top with pork. Add tomatoes, water, chili powder, salt and coriander. Cover; cook on LOW 7 to 9 hours.

Makes 6 servings

Nutrition Information: Serving Size about 1¹/₄ cups, Calories 243, Total Fat 4g, Saturated Fat 1g, Protein 25g, Carbohydrate 26g, Cholesterol 60mg, Dietary Fiber 5g, Sodium 494mg

Pork Chops with Dried Fruit and Onions

6 bone-in end-cut pork chops (about 2½ pounds)

Salt and black pepper (optional)

3 tablespoons vegetable oil

2 medium yellow onions, diced

2 cloves garlic, minced

¼ teaspoon dried sage

¾ cup quartered pitted dried plums

¾ cup chopped mixed dried fruit

3 cups unsweetened unfiltered apple juice

1 whole bay leaf

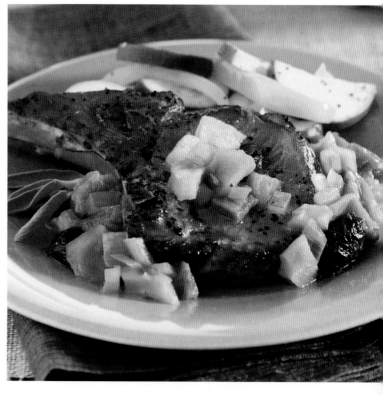

1. Season pork chops with salt and pepper, if desired. Heat oil in large skillet over medium-high heat. Add pork in batches; cook 5 to 7 minutes on each side or until browned. Remove to **CROCK-POT®** slow cooker.

2. Add onions to same skillet; cook and stir 3 to 5 minutes or until tender. Add garlic; cook 30 seconds. Sprinkle with sage. Add plums, dried fruit and apple juice; bring to a boil over high heat. Reduce heat to low; simmer and stir 3 minutes. Pour mixture over pork. Add bay leaf.

3. Cover; cook on LOW 3½ to 4 hours. Remove and discard bay leaf. To serve, spoon fruit and cooking liquid over pork chops.

Makes 6 servings

Nutrition Information: Serving Size 1 pork chop and ½ cup fruit and onions, Calories 359, Total Fat 11g, Saturated Fat 3g, Protein 24g, Carbohydrate 41g, Cholesterol 63mg, Dietary Fiber 3g, Sodium 91mg

Pork Main Dishes

Pork and Tomato Ragoût

  2 pounds lean pork top loin roast, cut into 1-inch pieces

  ¼ cup all-purpose flour

  2 tablespoons olive oil

1¼ cups dry white wine

  2 pounds red potatoes, cut into ½-inch pieces

  1 can (about 14 ounces) diced tomatoes

  1 cup finely chopped yellow onion

  1 cup water

  ½ cup finely chopped celery

  2 cloves garlic, minced

  ½ teaspoon black pepper

  1 cinnamon stick

  3 tablespoons chopped fresh parsley

Tip

Vegetables such as potatoes and carrots can sometimes take longer to cook in a **CROCK-POT**® slow cooker than meat. Place evenly cut vegetables along the sides of the **CROCK-POT**® slow cooker when possible.

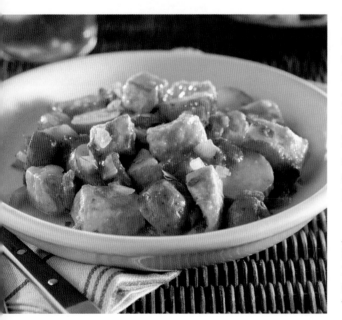

1. Toss pork with flour in large bowl. Heat oil in large skillet over medium-high heat. Add pork; cook 6 to 8 minutes or until browned on all sides. Remove pork to **CROCK-POT**® slow cooker.

2. Add wine to skillet, stirring to scrape up any browned bits. Pour into **CROCK-POT**® slow cooker.

3. Add potatoes, tomatoes, onion, water, celery, garlic, pepper and cinnamon stick to **CROCK-POT**® slow cooker. Cover; cook on LOW 6 to 8 hours or until pork and potatoes are tender. Remove and discard cinnamon stick. Top with parsley.

Makes 8 servings

Nutrition Information: Serving Size about 1¼ cups, Calories 323, Total Fat 8g, Saturated Fat 2g, Protein 29g, Carbohydrate 27g, Cholesterol 71mg, Dietary Fiber 3g, Sodium 212mg

Pork Chops à l'Orange

- **1 tablespoon extra virgin olive oil**
- **8 lean bone-in center-cut pork loin chops**
- **⅓ cup orange juice**
- **2 tablespoons honey**
- **1 teaspoon salt**
- **1 teaspoon packed brown sugar**
- **1 teaspoon grated orange peel**
- **¼ cup water**
- **2 tablespoons cornstarch**

1. Heat oil in large skillet over medium-high heat. Add pork in batches; cook 1 to 2 minutes on each side or until browned.

2. Combine orange juice, honey, salt, brown sugar and orange peel in **CROCK-POT®** slow cooker. Add chops; turn to coat. Cover; cook on LOW 6 to 8 hours.

3. Remove pork to large plate. Turn **CROCK-POT®** slow cooker to HIGH. Stir water into cornstarch in small bowl until smooth. Whisk into **CROCK-POT®** slow cooker. Cover; cook on HIGH 15 minutes or until thickened.

Makes 8 servings

Nutrition Information: Serving Size 1 pork chop and 1½ tablespoons sauce, Calories 197, Total Fat 7g, Saturated Fat 2g, Protein 23g, Carbohydrate 7g, Cholesterol 63mg, Dietary Fiber 0g, Sodium 347mg

Pork Main Dishes

Lemon Pork Chops

1 tablespoon vegetable oil

4 lean boneless pork loin chops

3 cans (8 ounces *each*) no-salt-added tomato sauce

1 large yellow onion, quartered and sliced (optional)

1 large green bell pepper, cut into strips

1 tablespoon lemon-pepper seasoning

1 tablespoon Worcestershire sauce

1 large lemon, quartered, plus additional for garnish

Tip

Browning pork before adding it to the **CROCK-POT®** slow cooker helps reduce the fat. Just remember to drain off the fat in the skillet before transferring the pork to the **CROCK-POT®** slow cooker.

1. Heat oil in large skillet over medium-low heat. Add pork chops; cook 3 to 5 minutes or until browned on both sides. Drain fat. Remove pork to **CROCK-POT®** slow cooker.

2. Combine tomato sauce, onion, if desired, bell pepper, lemon-pepper seasoning and Worcestershire sauce in medium bowl. Add to **CROCK-POT®** slow cooker.

3. Squeeze juice from 4 lemon quarters over sauce mixture; drop squeezed lemons into **CROCK-POT®** slow cooker. Cover; cook on LOW 6 to 8 hours or until pork is tender. Remove squeezed lemons before serving. Garnish with additional lemon quarters.

Makes 4 servings

Nutrition Information: Serving Size 1 pork chop and about ¹⁄₂ cup sauce, Calories 279, Total Fat 10g, Saturated Fat 2g, Protein 26g, Carbohydrate 21g, Cholesterol 63mg, Dietary Fiber 4g, Sodium 332mg

Ham with Fruited Bourbon Sauce

1 **fully cooked bone-in ham (about 6 pounds)**

¾ cup packed dark brown sugar

½ cup raisins

½ cup apple juice

1 teaspoon ground cinnamon

¼ teaspoon red pepper flakes

⅓ cup dried cherries

¼ cup bourbon, rum or apple juice

¼ cup cornstarch

1. Coat inside of **CROCK-POT®** slow cooker with nonstick cooking spray. Add ham, cut side up. Combine brown sugar, raisins, apple juice, cinnamon and red pepper flakes in small bowl; stir to blend. Pour over ham. Cover; cook on LOW 9 to 10 hours or on HIGH 4½ to 5 hours. Add cherries 30 minutes before end of cooking time.

2. Remove ham to cutting board. Cover loosely with foil; let stand 10 to 15 minutes before slicing.

3. Meanwhile, pour cooking liquid into large measuring cup. Let stand 5 minutes; skim and discard fat. Return cooking liquid to **CROCK-POT®** slow cooker.

4. Stir bourbon into cornstarch in small bowl until smooth. Whisk into cooking liquid. Cover; cook on HIGH 15 minutes or until sauce is thickened. Serve ham with sauce.

Makes 12 servings

Nutrition Information: Serving Size ¹⁄₁₂ ham and about ¼ cup sauce, Calories 423, Total Fat 12g, Saturated Fat 4g, Protein 47g, Carbohydrate 26g, Cholesterol 154mg, Dietary Fiber 1g, Sodium 131mg

Pork Main Dishes

Andouille and Cabbage Crock

1   **pound andouille sausage, cut into 3- to 4-inch pieces**

1   **small head cabbage, cut into 8 wedges (about 1 pound total)**

1   **medium onion, cut into ½-inch wedges**

3   **medium carrots, quartered lengthwise, and cut into 3-inch pieces**

8   **new potatoes, cut in half (about 1 pound total)**

½   **cup apple juice**

1   **can (about 14 ounces) 99% fat-free reduced-sodium chicken broth**

    Honey mustard and crusty rolls (optional)

Tip
Andouille is a spicy, smoked pork sausage. Feel free to substitute your favorite smoked sausage or kielbasa.

1. Cook sausage in large skillet coated with nonstick cooking spray over medium-high heat. Stir sausage frequently until brown on both sides. Remove from heat; set aside.

2. Coat inside of **CROCK-POT®** slow cooker with cooking spray. Place all ingredients except honey mustard and rolls in **CROCK-POT®** slow cooker, with sausage on top. Cover; cook on HIGH 3½ hours. Stir gently, making sure vegetables are covered with liquid. Cover; cook on HIGH 30 minutes or until cabbage is tender. Remove with slotted spoon to large serving platter. Serve with honey mustard and crusty rolls, if desired.

Makes about 8 servings

Nutrition Information: Serving Size 1½ cups, Calories 290, Total Fat 11g, Saturated Fat 4g, Protein 14g, Carbohydrate 38g, Cholesterol 32mg, Dietary Fiber 7g, Sodium 588mg

Cajun-Style Country Ribs

- **2 cups baby carrots**
- **1 medium onion, coarsely chopped**
- **1 green bell pepper, cut into 1-inch pieces**
- **1 red bell pepper, cut into 1-inch pieces**
- **2 teaspoons minced garlic**
- **2 tablespoons Creole seasoning, divided**
- **3 pounds country-style pork ribs, trimmed and cut into individual portions**
- **1 can (about 14 ounces) no-salt-added stewed tomatoes, undrained**
- **2 tablespoons water**
- **1 tablespoon cornstarch**
- **Hot cooked rice (optional)**

1. Combine carrots, onion, bell peppers, garlic and 2 teaspoons seasoning in **CROCK-POT®** slow cooker; mix well.

2. Sprinkle ribs with 1 tablespoon seasoning; place in **CROCK-POT®** slow cooker. Pour tomatoes over ribs. Cover; cook on LOW 6 to 8 hours.

3. Remove ribs and vegetables from **CROCK-POT®** slow cooker with slotted spoon. Turn off heat. Let liquid stand 15 minutes; skim off fat.

4. Turn **CROCK-POT®** slow cooker to HIGH. Stir water into cornstarch and remaining 1 teaspoon seasoning in small bowl until smooth. Whisk into **CROCK-POT®** slow cooker. Cook, uncovered, on HIGH 15 minutes or until thickened. Return ribs and vegetables to sauce; carefully stir to coat. Serve with rice, if desired.

Makes 8 servings

Nutrition Information: Serving Size ⅛ ribs and about ½ cup vegetables, Calories 286, Total Fat 10g, Saturated Fat 2g, Protein 36g, Carbohydrate 10g, Cholesterol 126mg, Dietary Fiber 2g, Sodium 587mg

Poultry Main Dishes

East Indian Curried Chicken with Capers and Brown Rice

2	**cups ripe plum tomatoes, diced**
1	**cup artichoke hearts, drained and chopped**
1	**cup 99% fat-free chicken broth**
1	**medium red onion, chopped**
1/3	**cup dry white wine**
1/4	**cup capers, drained**
2	**tablespoons quick-cooking tapioca**
2	**teaspoons curry powder**
1/2	**teaspoon ground thyme**
1/4	**teaspoon salt**
1/4	**teaspoon black pepper**
1 1/2	**pounds boneless, skinless chicken breasts**
4	**cups cooked brown rice**

1. Combine tomatoes, artichokes, broth, onion, wine and capers in **CROCK-POT**® slow cooker.

2. Combine tapioca, curry powder, thyme, salt and pepper in small bowl. Add to **CROCK-POT**® slow cooker. Stir well to combine. Add chicken. Spoon sauce over chicken to coat. Cover; cook on LOW 7 to 9 hours or on HIGH 3 to 4 hours.

3. Serve chicken and vegetables over rice. Spoon sauce over chicken.

Makes 6 servings

Nutrition Information: Serving Size about 1 1/2 cups, Calories 327, Total Fat 4g, Saturated Fat 1g, Protein 30g, Carbohydrate 41g, Cholesterol 73mg, Dietary Fiber 4g, Sodium 648mg

Cuban-Style Curried Turkey

 2 **tablespoons all-purpose flour**

 ½ **teaspoon salt**

 ¼ **teaspoon black pepper**

 1 **pound boneless turkey breast or turkey tenderloins, cut into 1-inch cubes**

 2 **tablespoons vegetable oil, divided**

 1 **small yellow onion, chopped**

 1 **clove garlic, minced**

 1 **can (about 15 ounces) reduced-sodium black beans, rinsed and drained**

 1 **can (about 14 ounces) no-salt-added diced tomatoes**

 ½ **cup fat-free reduced-sodium chicken broth**

 ⅓ **cup raisins**

 ¼ **teaspoon curry powder**

 ⅛ **teaspoon red pepper flakes**

 1 **tablespoon lime juice**

 1 **tablespoon minced fresh cilantro (optional)**

 1 **tablespoon minced green onion (optional)**

 2 **cups cooked rice (optional)**

1. Combine flour, salt and black pepper in large resealable food storage bag. Add turkey; shake to coat. Heat 1 tablespoon oil in large skillet over medium heat. Add turkey; cook 6 to 8 minutes or until browned on all sides. Remove to **CROCK-POT®** slow cooker.

2. Heat remaining 1 tablespoon oil in same skillet over medium heat. Add onion; cook and stir 3 minutes or until tender. Stir in garlic; cook 30 seconds. Remove to **CROCK-POT®** slow cooker.

3. Stir in beans, tomatoes, broth, raisins, curry powder and red pepper flakes. Cover; cook on LOW 4 to 6 hours. Stir in lime juice. Garnish with cilantro and green onion. Serve over rice, if desired.

Makes 4 servings

Nutrition Information: Serving Size about 1¾ cups, Calories 328, Total Fat 8g, Saturated Fat 1g, Protein 32g, Carbohydrate 34g, Cholesterol 56mg, Dietary Fiber 6g, Sodium 690mg

Poultry Main Dishes

Chicken Gumbo over Rice

- **2 tablespoons olive oil**
- **½ pound Italian sausage, cut into ¼-inch slices**
- **¼ cup all-purpose flour**
- **1 pound boneless, skinless chicken breasts, cut into ½-inch slices**
- **1 cup chopped yellow onion**
- **1 cup chopped celery**
- **1 cup diced green bell pepper**
- **2 tablespoons minced jalapeño or serrano peppers***
- **1 teaspoon paprika**
- **1½ cups frozen okra**
- **1 cup 99% fat-free chicken broth**
- **½ cup dry white wine**
- **2 cups cooked brown rice**

Jalapeño and serrano peppers can sting and irritate the skin, so wear rubber gloves when handling peppers and do not touch your eyes.

1. Heat oil in large skillet over medium heat. Add sausage; cook and stir 10 minutes or until browned on both sides. Remove to large paper towel-lined plate using slotted spoon.

2. Add flour to skillet; cook and stir until flour becomes dark brown but not burnt. Add chicken, onion, celery, bell pepper, jalapeño peppers and paprika; cook and stir 7 to 8 minutes or until vegetables are soft. Remove to **CROCK-POT®** slow cooker. Stir in sausage, okra, broth and wine. Cover; cook on LOW 7 to 8 hours or on HIGH 4 to 6 hours. Serve over rice.

Makes 6 servings

Nutrition Information: Serving Size about 1¼ cups, Calories 441, Total Fat 24g, Saturated Fat 7g, Protein 25g, Carbohydrate 26g, Cholesterol 77mg, Dietary Fiber 2g, Sodium 608mg

Creole Vegetables and Chicken

  2 **cups chopped green bell peppers**

  1 **can (about 14 ounces) no-salt-added diced tomatoes**

  1 **cup chopped yellow onion**

  8 **ounces frozen cut okra, thawed**

  1 **cup fat-free reduced-sodium chicken broth**

  ¾ **cup sliced celery**

  2 **teaspoons Worcestershire sauce**

  1 **teaspoon dried thyme**

  1 **whole bay leaf**

  1 **tablespoon extra virgin olive oil**

  1 **pound chicken tenders, cut into 1-inch pieces**

1½ **teaspoons sugar**

  ¾ **teaspoon Creole seasoning**

     Hot pepper sauce (optional)

  ¼ **cup chopped fresh Italian parsley**

Tip

To slightly thicken stews in the **CROCK-POT®** slow cooker, remove the solid foods and leave the cooking liquid in the stoneware. Stir ¼ cup cold water into 2 to 4 tablespoons cornstarch in small bowl until smooth. Whisk into the **CROCK-POT®** slow cooker. Cover; cook on HIGH 15 minutes or until thickened.

1. Coat inside of **CROCK-POT®** slow cooker with nonstick cooking spray. Add bell peppers, tomatoes, onion, okra, broth, celery, Worcestershire sauce, thyme and bay leaf.

2. Heat oil in medium skillet over medium-high heat. Add chicken; cook and stir 6 minutes or until lightly browned. Remove to **CROCK-POT®** slow cooker. Cover; cook on LOW 9 hours or on HIGH 4½ hours. Remove and discard bay leaf.

3. Stir in sugar, Creole seasoning and hot pepper sauce, if desired. Cover; cook on HIGH 15 minutes. Stir in parsley.

Makes 8 servings

Nutrition Information: Serving Size about 1½ cups, Calories 209, Total Fat 11g, Saturated Fat 2g, Protein 10g, Carbohydrate 18g, Cholesterol 23mg, Dietary Fiber 3g, Sodium 375mg

Poultry Main Dishes

Curry Chicken with Mango and Red Pepper

6 boneless, skinless chicken thighs or breasts

Salt and black pepper (optional)

Nonstick cooking spray

1 bag (8 ounces) frozen mango pieces, thawed and drained

2 red bell peppers, diced

⅓ cup raisins

1 shallot, thinly sliced

¾ cup 99% fat-free chicken broth

1 tablespoon cider vinegar

2 cloves garlic, crushed

4 thin slices fresh ginger

1 teaspoon ground cumin

½ teaspoon curry powder

½ teaspoon whole cloves

¼ teaspoon ground red pepper (optional)

Fresh cilantro (optional)

1. Season chicken with salt and black pepper, if desired. Heat cooking spray in large skillet over medium heat. Add chicken; cook 3 minutes per side or until lightly browned. Remove to **CROCK-POT®** slow cooker.

2. Add mango, bell peppers, raisins and shallot. Combine broth, vinegar, garlic, ginger, cumin, curry powder, cloves and ground red pepper, if desired, in small bowl; pour over chicken. Cover; cook on LOW 6 to 8 hours or on HIGH 3 to 4 hours. To serve, spoon mangos, raisins and cooking liquid evenly onto chicken. Garnish with cilantro.

Makes 4 servings

Nutrition Information: Serving Size about 1½ cups, Calories 315, Total Fat 5g, Saturated Fat 1g, Protein 40g, Carbohydrate 26g, Cholesterol 113mg, Dietary Fiber 3g, Sodium 387mg

Quatro Frijoles con Pollo Cantaro

- **1 cup pitted black olives, drained**
- **1 pound boneless, skinless chicken breasts, cut into 1-inch pieces**
- **1 can (about 15 ounces) no-salt-added chickpeas, rinsed and drained**
- **1 can (about 15 ounces) no-salt-added Great Northern beans, rinsed and drained**
- **1 can (about 15 ounces) no-salt-added cannellini beans, rinsed and drained**
- **1 can (about 15 ounces) no-salt-added red kidney beans, rinsed and drained**
- **1 can (7 ounces) chopped mild green chiles, drained**
- **2 cups 99% fat-free chicken broth**
- **1 tablespoon canola oil**
- **1 cup minced yellow onion**
- **2 teaspoons minced garlic**
- **1½ teaspoons ground cumin**
- **Hot pepper sauce (optional)**
- **Salt and black pepper (optional)**
- **2 cups crushed corn chips (optional)**
- **1½ cups (6 ounces) shredded Monterey Jack cheese (optional)**

1. Combine olives, chicken, chickpeas, beans, chiles and broth in **CROCK-POT®** slow cooker; stir to blend.

2. Heat oil in large skillet over medium-high heat. Add onion, garlic and cumin; cook and stir 3 to 5 minutes or until onion is tender. Remove to **CROCK-POT®** slow cooker. Cover; cook on LOW 4 to 5 hours, checking liquid halfway through cooking time and adding water if necessary.

3. Stir in hot pepper sauce, salt and pepper, if desired. Top each serving with chips and cheese, if desired.

Makes 6 servings

Nutrition Information: Serving Size 1½ cups, Calories 417, Total Fat 10g, Saturated Fat 1g, Protein 31g, Carbohydrate 50g, Cholesterol 48mg, Dietary Fiber 14g, Sodium 741mg

Chicken Tangier

- **2 tablespoons dried oregano**
- **2 teaspoons seasoning salt**
- **2 teaspoons minced garlic**
- **¼ teaspoon black pepper**
- **3 pounds boneless, skinless chicken breasts**
- **1 lemon, thinly sliced**
- **½ cup dry white wine**
- **2 tablespoons olive oil**
- **1 cup pitted prunes**
- **¼ cup raisins**
- **½ cup pitted green olives**
- **2 tablespoons capers**
- **Cooked noodles or rice**
- **Chopped fresh parsley or cilantro (optional)**

Tip

It may seem like a lot, but this recipe really does call for 2 tablespoons dried oregano in order to more accurately represent the powerfully seasoned flavors of Morocco.

1. Stir together oregano, salt, garlic and pepper in small bowl. Rub onto chicken, being certain to coat all sides.

2. Coat inside of **CROCK-POT®** slow cooker with nonstick cooking spray. Arrange chicken inside, tucking lemon slices between pieces. Pour wine over chicken and sprinkle with olive oil. Add prunes, raisins, olives and capers. Cover; cook on LOW 7 to 8 hours or on HIGH 4 to 5 hours.

3. Serve over cooked noodles or rice and sprinkle with parsley, if desired.

Makes 8 servings

Nutrition Information: Serving Size about 1 cup, Calories 334, Total Fat 10g, Saturated Fat 1g, Protein 37g, Carbohydrate 20g, Cholesterol 109mg, Dietary Fiber 2g, Sodium 742mg

Braised Italian Chicken with Tomatoes and Olives

- **2 pounds boneless, skinless chicken breasts**
- **¼ teaspoon kosher salt**
- **½ teaspoon black pepper**
- **½ cup all-purpose flour**
- **Nonstick cooking spray**
- **1 can (about 14 ounces) no-salt-added diced tomatoes, drained**
- **⅓ cup dry red wine**
- **⅓ cup quartered pitted kalamata olives**
- **1 clove garlic, minced**
- **1 teaspoon chopped fresh rosemary**
- **½ teaspoon red pepper flakes**
- **Hot cooked linguini or spaghetti (optional)**
- **Grated Parmesan cheese (optional)**
- **Sprigs fresh rosemary (optional)**

1. Season chicken with salt and black pepper. Place flour in shallow plate. Add chicken; coat with flour on both sides.

2. Heat cooking spray in large skillet over medium heat. Add chicken; cook in batches 6 to 8 minutes or until browned on all sides. Remove to **CROCK-POT®** slow cooker using slotted spoon. Add tomatoes, wine, olives and garlic. Cover; cook on LOW 4 to 5 hours.

3. Stir in chopped rosemary and red pepper flakes. Cover; cook on LOW 1 hour. Serve over linguini, if desired. Garnish with cheese and rosemary sprigs.

Makes 4 servings

Nutrition Information: Serving Size about 1¼ cups, Calories 374, Total Fat 7g, Saturated Fat 1g, Protein 51g, Carbohydrate 18g, Cholesterol 145mg, Dietary Fiber 1g, Sodium 808mg

Poultry Main Dishes

Slow Cooker Turkey Breast

  1 turkey breast (3 pounds)*
    Garlic powder
    Paprika
    Dried parsley flakes

***Unless you have a 5-, 6- or 7-quart CROCK-POT® slow cooker, cut any meat larger than
2¹⁄₂ pounds in half so it cooks completely.***

1. Season turkey with garlic powder, paprika and parsley. Place in **CROCK-POT®** slow cooker. Cover; cook on LOW 6 to 8 hours or until internal temperature reaches 170°F.

2. Remove turkey to cutting board. Cover loosely with foil; let stand 10 to 15 minutes before slicing.

Makes 6 servings

Nutrition Information: Serving Size ¹⁄₆ turkey breast, Calories 240, Total Fat 3g, Saturated Fat 1g, Protein 53g, Carbohydrate 0g, Cholesterol 111mg, Dietary Fiber 0g, Sodium 122mg

Italian-Style Turkey Sausage

  1 package (about 1 pound) lean Italian turkey sausage, cut into 1-inch pieces
  1 can (about 15 ounces) no-salt-added pinto beans, rinsed and drained
  1 cup low-sodium meatless pasta sauce
  1 medium green bell pepper, cut into strips
  1 small yellow onion, halved and sliced
 ¹⁄₂ teaspoon salt
 ¹⁄₄ teaspoon black pepper
    Fresh basil leaves (optional)
    Italian bread (optional)

1. Brown sausage in large skillet over medium-high heat 6 to 8 minutes, stirring to break up meat. Drain fat.

2. Place sausage, beans, pasta sauce, bell pepper, onion, salt and black pepper in **CROCK-POT®** slow cooker. Cover; cook on LOW 4 to 6 hours or on HIGH 2 to 3 hours. Garnish with basil. Serve with bread, if desired.

Makes 5 servings

Nutrition Information: Serving Size 1 link sausage and ¹⁄₄ cup sauce, Calories 202, Total Fat 9g, Saturated Fat 3g, Protein 17g, Carbohydrate 15g, Cholesterol 45mg, Dietary Fiber 4g, Sodium 722mg

**Slow Cooker
Turkey Breast**

Hearty Cassoulet

- **1 tablespoon olive oil**
- **1 large yellow onion, finely chopped**
- **1 pound boneless, skinless chicken breasts, chopped**
- **¼ pound smoked turkey sausage, finely diced**
- **3 cloves garlic, minced**
- **1 teaspoon dried thyme**
- **½ teaspoon black pepper**
- **¼ cup tomato paste**
- **2 tablespoons water**
- **3 cans (about 15 ounces *each*) Great Northern beans, rinsed and drained**
- **½ cup dry bread crumbs**
- **3 tablespoons minced fresh Italian parsley**

> ### Tip
> When preparing ingredients for the **CROCK-POT®** slow cooker, cut into uniform pieces so that everything cooks evenly.

1. Heat oil in large skillet over medium heat. Add onion; cook and stir 5 minutes or until onion is tender. Add chicken, sausage, garlic, thyme and pepper; cook and stir 5 minutes or until chicken and sausage are browned.

2. Remove skillet from heat. Stir in tomato paste and water until blended. Place chicken mixture and beans in **CROCK-POT®** slow cooker. Cover; cook on LOW 4 to 4½ hours. Combine bread crumbs and parsley in small bowl; sprinkle evenly over each serving.

Makes 8 servings

Nutrition Information: Serving Size about 1 cup, Calories 283, Total Fat 6g, Saturated Fat 1g, Protein 24g, Carbohydrate 31g, Cholesterol 44mg, Dietary Fiber 10g, Sodium 744mg

Forty-Clove Chicken

1	**cut-up whole chicken (about 3 pounds)**
	Salt and black pepper (optional)
1	**tablespoon olive oil**
40	**cloves garlic (about 2 bulbs)**
4	**stalks celery, sliced**
¼	**cup dry white wine**
2	**tablespoons chopped fresh Italian parsley** *or* **2 teaspoons dried parsley flakes**
2	**tablespoons dry vermouth**
2	**teaspoons dried basil**
1	**teaspoon dried oregano**
	Pinch red pepper flakes
	Juice and peel of 1 lemon

1. Remove skin from chicken; season with salt and black pepper, if desired. Heat oil in large skillet over medium heat. Add chicken; cook 3 to 5 minutes or until browned on all sides. Remove to large bowl.

2. Add garlic, celery, wine, parsley, vermouth, basil, oregano and red pepper flakes to chicken in large bowl; toss to coat. Place chicken mixture in **CROCK-POT®** slow cooker. Sprinkle lemon juice and peel over chicken. Cover; cook on LOW 6 hours.

Makes 6 servings

Nutrition Information: Serving Size ⅙ chicken and sauce, Calories 201, Total Fat 6g, Saturated Fat 1g, Protein 25g, Carbohydrate 9g, Cholesterol 77mg, Dietary Fiber 1g, Sodium 111mg

Poultry Main Dishes

Turkey Piccata

2½ **tablespoons all-purpose flour**

¼ **teaspoon salt**

¼ **teaspoon black pepper**

1 **pound turkey breast, cut into strips**

1 **tablespoon unsalted butter**

1 **tablespoon olive oil**

½ **cup 99% fat-free chicken broth**

Grated peel of 1 lemon

2 **teaspoons lemon juice**

2 **tablespoons finely chopped fresh Italian parsley**

2 **cups hot cooked rice (optional)**

1. Combine flour, salt and pepper in large resealable food storage bag. Add turkey strips; shake to coat. Heat butter and oil in large skillet over medium-high heat. Add turkey; cook 3 to 5 minutes or until browned on all sides. Arrange in single layer in **CROCK-POT®** slow cooker.

2. Pour broth into skillet, stirring to scrape up any browned bits. Pour into **CROCK-POT®** slow cooker. Add lemon peel and juice. Cover; cook on LOW 2 hours. Sprinkle with parsley. Serve over rice, if desired.

Makes 4 servings

Nutrition Information: Serving Size about 1¼ cups, Calories 199, Total Fat 8g, Saturated Fat 3g, Protein 27g, Carbohydrate 4g, Cholesterol 63mg, Dietary Fiber 0g, Sodium 386mg

Barley and Sausage Gumbo

- **1 small yellow onion, chopped**
- **1 large green bell pepper, chopped**
- **1 cup frozen sliced okra, thawed**
- **1 medium stalk celery, chopped**
- **1 clove garlic, minced**
- **1 cup reduced-sodium chicken broth**
- **1 cup no-salt-added tomato purée**
- **¼ cup uncooked pearl barley**
- **1 teaspoon dried oregano**
- **¼ teaspoon salt (optional)**
- **⅛ teaspoon red pepper flakes**
- **2 reduced-fat chicken andouille sausages (3 ounces *each*), sliced ½ inch thick**

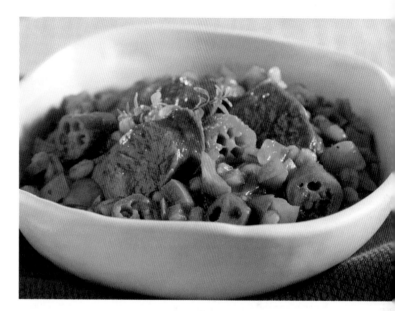

Place onion, bell pepper, okra, celery and garlic in **CROCK-POT®** slow cooker. Add broth, tomato purée, barley, oregano, salt, if desired, and red pepper flakes; stir to blend. Stir in sausages. Cover; cook on LOW 5 to 6 hours. Turn off heat. Let stand 5 minutes before serving.

Makes 4 servings

Nutrition Information: Serving Size about 1¼ cups, Calories 169, Total Fat 4g, Saturated Fat 1g, Protein 12g, Carbohydrate 23g, Cholesterol 33mg, Dietary Fiber 6g, Sodium 409mg

Spicy Turkey with Citrus au Jus

1 **turkey breast (about 4 pounds)***

¼ **cup (½ stick) unsalted butter, softened**

   Grated peel of 1 lemon

1 **teaspoon chili powder**

¼ **to ½ teaspoon black pepper**

⅛ **to ¼ teaspoon red pepper flakes**

1 **tablespoon lemon juice**

*Unless you have a 5-, 6- or 7-quart CROCK-POT® slow cooker, cut any meat larger than 2½ pounds in half so it cooks completely.

1. Coat inside of **CROCK-POT®** slow cooker with nonstick cooking spray. Add turkey breast.

2. Combine butter, lemon peel, chili powder, black pepper and red pepper flakes in small bowl; stir until well blended. Spread mixture over top and sides of turkey. Cover; cook on LOW 4 to 5 hours or on HIGH 2½ to 3 hours or until cooked through.

3. Remove turkey to cutting board. Cover loosely with foil; let stand 10 to 15 minutes before slicing. Stir lemon juice into cooking liquid. Strain; discard solids. Turn off heat. Let mixture stand 15 minutes. Skim and discard excess fat. Serve sauce with turkey.

Makes 8 servings

Nutrition Information: Serving Size ⅛ turkey breast, Calories 304, Total Fat 7g, Saturated Fat 4g, Protein 56g, Carbohydrate 0g, Cholesterol 156mg, Dietary Fiber 0g, Sodium 115mg

Rice and Chicken Pilaf

- **1 teaspoon olive oil**
- **1 medium red bell pepper, chopped**
- **1 stalk celery, trimmed and chopped**
- **1 clove garlic, minced**
- **½ cup uncooked converted rice**
- **¼ teaspoon salt**
- **⅛ teaspoon black pepper**
- **⅛ teaspoon crushed dried thyme**
  Dash ground red pepper
- **1 pound boneless, skinless chicken breasts, cut into 1-inch pieces**
- **1 cup fat-free reduced-sodium chicken broth**
- **1 large green onion, finely chopped**
- **¼ cup grated Parmesan cheese**

1. Heat oil in large skillet over medium-high heat. Add bell pepper, celery and garlic; cook and stir 3 to 4 minutes or until vegetables are softened.

2. Add rice; cook and stir 1 minute until rice is glossy. Stir in salt, black pepper, thyme and ground red pepper. Remove to **CROCK-POT®** slow cooker.

3. Stir in chicken and broth. Cover; cook on LOW 3½ hours. Stir in green onion. Cover; cook on LOW 15 minutes. Sprinkle each serving evenly with Parmesan cheese.

Makes 6 servings

Nutrition Information: Serving Size 1 cup, Calories 222, Total Fat 11g, Saturated Fat 4g, Protein 16g, Carbohydrate 14g, Cholesterol 51mg, Dietary Fiber 1g, Sodium 233mg

Tuscan Pasta

1 pound boneless, skinless chicken breasts, cut into 1-inch pieces

2 cans (about 14 ounces *each*) Italian-style stewed tomatoes, undrained

1 can (about 15 ounces) red kidney beans, rinsed and drained

1 can (15 ounces) tomato sauce

1 cup water

1 jar (4½ ounces) sliced mushrooms, drained

1 medium green bell pepper, chopped

½ cup chopped yellow onion

½ cup chopped celery

4 cloves garlic, minced

1 teaspoon Italian seasoning

6 ounces uncooked thin spaghetti, broken in half

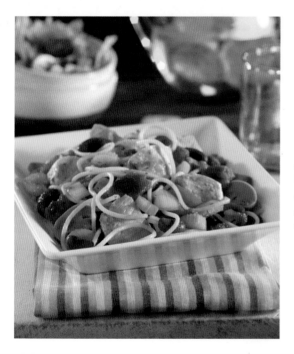

1. Combine chicken, tomatoes, beans, tomato sauce, water, mushrooms, bell pepper, onion, celery, garlic and Italian seasoning in **CROCK-POT®** slow cooker. Cover; cook on LOW 4 hours or until vegetables are tender.

2. Turn **CROCK-POT®** slow cooker to HIGH. Stir in spaghetti. Cover; cook on HIGH 35 minutes or until pasta is tender.

Makes 8 servings

Nutrition Information: Serving Size about 1½ cups, Calories 408, Total Fat 7g, Saturated Fat 2g, Protein 28g, Carbohydrate 60g, Cholesterol 36mg, Dietary Fiber 16g, Sodium 565mg

Turkey Ropa Vieja

- **12 ounces turkey tenderloin (2 large or 3 small) or boneless, skinless chicken thighs**
- **1 can (8 ounces) no-salt-added tomato sauce**
- **2 medium tomatoes, chopped**
- **1 small yellow onion, thinly sliced**
- **1 small green bell pepper, chopped**
- **4 pimiento-stuffed green olives, sliced**
- **1 clove garlic, minced**
- **¾ teaspoon ground cumin**
- **½ teaspoon dried oregano**
- **⅛ teaspoon black pepper**
- **2 teaspoons lemon juice**
- **¼ teaspoon salt (optional)**
- **1 cup hot cooked rice (optional)**
- **1 cup cooked black beans (optional)**

1. Place turkey in **CROCK-POT®** slow cooker. Add tomato sauce, tomatoes, onion, bell pepper, olives, garlic, cumin, oregano and black pepper. Cover; cook on LOW 6 to 7 hours.

2. Remove turkey to cutting board; shred with two forks. Return turkey to **CROCK-POT®** slow cooker. Stir in lemon juice and salt, if desired. Serve with rice and black beans, if desired.

Makes 4 servings

Nutrition Information: Serving Size about 1½ cups, Calories 146, Total Fat 2g, Saturated Fat 0g, Protein 22g, Carbohydrate 11g, Cholesterol 42mg, Dietary Fiber 2g, Sodium 182mg

Autumn Herbed Chicken with Fennel and Squash

- **3 pounds boneless, skinless chicken breasts**
- **Salt and black pepper (optional)**
- **¼ cup all-purpose flour**
- **2 tablespoons olive oil**
- **1 fennel bulb, thinly sliced**
- **½ butternut squash, peeled, seeded and cut into ¾-inch cubes**
- **¾ cup walnuts (optional)**
- **¾ cup 99% fat-free chicken broth**
- **½ cup unsweetened apple juice**
- **1 teaspoon dried thyme**
- **Cooked rice or pasta (optional)**
- **¼ cup fresh basil, sliced into ribbons (optional)**
- **2 teaspoons fresh rosemary, finely minced (optional)**

1. Season chicken with salt and pepper, if desired. Add flour to large resealable food storage bag. Add chicken; shake to coat. Heat oil in large skillet over medium heat. Add chicken in batches; cook 3 to 5 minutes on each side or until browned. Remove to **CROCK-POT®** slow cooker.

2. Stir in fennel, squash, walnuts, if desired, broth, apple juice and thyme. Cover; cook on LOW 5 to 7 hours or on HIGH 2½ to 4½ hours. Serve over rice, if desired. Garnish with basil and rosemary.

Makes 6 servings

Nutrition Information: Serving Size makes about 1¼ cups, Calories 356, Total Fat 11g, Saturated Fat 2g, Protein 50g, Carbohydrate 14g, Cholesterol 145mg, Dietary Fiber 3g, Sodium 403mg

Mediterranean Chicken

- **1** tablespoon olive oil
- **2** pounds boneless, skinless chicken breasts
- **2** medium yellow onions, chopped
- **1** can (28 ounces) diced tomatoes
  Juice of 2 lemons
- **½** cup dry sherry
- **2** cinnamon sticks
- **2** tablespoons minced garlic
- **½** teaspoon black pepper
- **1** whole bay leaf
- **1** pound cooked egg noodles
- **½** cup feta cheese

1. Heat oil in large skillet. Add chicken; cook 3 to 5 minutes on each side or until browned.

2. Combine onions, tomatoes, lemon juice, sherry, cinnamon sticks, garlic, pepper and bay leaf in **CROCK-POT®** slow cooker; top with chicken. Cover; cook on LOW 8 to 10 hours or on HIGH 4 to 5 hours.

3. Remove and discard cinnamon sticks and bay leaf. Serve chicken and sauce over noodles. Sprinkle evenly with cheese just before serving.

Makes 8 servings

Nutrition Information: Serving Size about 1½ cups, Calories 432, Total Fat 8g, Saturated Fat 3g, Protein 34g, Carbohydrate 51g, Cholesterol 81mg, Dietary Fiber 3g, Sodium 440mg

Turkey Breast with Barley-Cranberry Stuffing

1 **fresh or thawed frozen bone-in turkey breast half (about 2 pounds), skinned**

2 **cups reduced-sodium chicken broth**

1 **cup uncooked quick-cooking barley**

1/2 **cup chopped yellow onion**

1/2 **cup dried cranberries**

2 **tablespoons slivered almonds, toasted***

1/2 **teaspoon rubbed sage**

1/2 **teaspoon garlic-pepper seasoning**

1/3 **cup finely chopped fresh parsley**

*To toast almonds, spread in single layer on baking sheet. Bake in preheated 350°F oven 8 to 10 minutes or until golden brown, stirring frequently.

1. Thaw turkey breast, if frozen. Remove skin and discard.

2. Combine broth, barley, onion, cranberries, almonds, sage and garlic-pepper seasoning in **CROCK-POT®** slow cooker.

3. Coat large nonstick skillet with cooking spray. Heat over medium heat until hot. Brown turkey breast on all sides; add to **CROCK-POT®** slow cooker. Cover; cook on LOW 4 to 6 hours.

4. Transfer turkey to cutting board; cover with foil to keep warm. Let stand 10 to 15 minutes before carving. Stir parsley into sauce mixture in **CROCK-POT®** slow cooker. Serve over sliced turkey and stuffing.

Makes 6 servings

Nutrition Information: Serving Size 1/6 turkey breast, Calories 379, Total Fat 12g, Saturated Fat 3g, Protein 35g, Carbohydrate 33g, Cholesterol 88mg, Dietary Fiber 7g, Sodium 306mg

Simple Coq au Vin

- **1 pound boneless, skinless chicken breasts**
- **Salt and black pepper (optional)**
- **2 tablespoons olive oil**
- **8 ounces mushrooms, sliced**
- **1 medium yellow onion, cut into rings**
- **½ cup dry red wine**
- **½ teaspoon dried basil**
- **½ teaspoon dried thyme**
- **½ teaspoon dried oregano**
- **Hot cooked rice (optional)**

1. Season chicken with salt and pepper, if desired. Heat oil in large skillet over medium-high heat. Add chicken; cook 3 to 5 minutes or until browned on all sides. Remove chicken to **CROCK-POT®** slow cooker.

2. Add mushrooms and onion to same skillet; cook and stir 5 minutes or until tender. Add wine, stirring to scrape up any brown bits. Add to **CROCK-POT®** slow cooker. Add basil, thyme and oregano. Cover; cook on LOW 8 to 10 hours or on HIGH 3 to 4 hours. Serve over rice, if desired.

Makes 4 servings

Nutrition Information: Serving Size about 1 cup chicken and sauce, Calories 245, Total Fat 11g, Saturated Fat 2g, Protein 25g, Carbohydrate 6g, Cholesterol 72mg, Dietary Fiber 1g, Sodium 138mg

Tip
Browning poultry before cooking it in the **CROCK-POT®** slow cooker isn't necessary, but it helps to enhance the flavor and adds an oven-roasted appearance to the finished dish.

Poultry Main Dishes

Herbed Artichoke Chicken

1½ **pounds boneless, skinless chicken breasts**

1 **can (about 14 ounces) no-salt-added diced tomatoes, drained**

1 **can (14 ounces) artichoke hearts in water, drained**

1 **small yellow onion, chopped**

1 **cup 99% fat-free reduced-sodium chicken broth**

½ **cup kalamata olives, pitted and sliced**

¼ **cup dry white wine**

3 **tablespoons quick-cooking tapioca**

1 **tablespoon chopped fresh Italian parsley**

2 **teaspoons curry powder**

1 **teaspoon dried sweet basil**

1 **teaspoon dried thyme**

½ **teaspoon salt**

½ **teaspoon black pepper**

Combine chicken, tomatoes, artichokes, onion, broth, olives, wine, tapioca, parsley, curry powder, basil, thyme, salt and pepper in **CROCK-POT®** slow cooker; stir to blend. Cover; cook on LOW 6 to 8 hours or on HIGH 3½ to 4 hours or until chicken is cooked through.

Makes 8 servings

Nutrition Information: Serving Size about 1½ cups, Calories 219, Total Fat 11g, Saturated Fat 3g, Protein 18g, Carbohydrate 13g, Cholesterol 54mg, Dietary Fiber 3g, Sodium 569mg

Fusilli Pizzaiola with Turkey Meatballs

- **2** **cans (about 14 ounces *each*) no-salt-added whole tomatoes**
- **1** **can (8 ounces) no-salt-added tomato sauce**
- **¼** **cup chopped yellow onion**
- **¼** **cup grated carrot**
- **2** **tablespoons no-salt-added tomato paste**
- **2** **tablespoons chopped fresh basil**
- **1** **clove garlic, minced**
- **½** **teaspoon dried thyme**
- **¼** **teaspoon sugar**
- **¼** **teaspoon black pepper, divided**
- **1** **whole bay leaf**
- **1** **pound 93% lean ground turkey breast**
- **1** **egg, lightly beaten**
- **1** **tablespoon fat-free (skim) milk**
- **¼** **cup Italian-seasoned dry bread crumbs**
- **2** **tablespoons chopped fresh parsley**
- **8** **ounces uncooked fusilli or other spiral-shaped pasta**

1. Combine tomatoes, tomato sauce, onion, carrot, tomato paste, basil, garlic, thyme, sugar, ⅛ teaspoon pepper and bay leaf in **CROCK-POT®** slow cooker. Break up tomatoes gently with wooden spoon. Cover; cook on LOW 4½ to 5 hours.

2. Prepare meatballs 45 minutes before end of cooking. Preheat oven to 350°F. Spray baking sheet with nonstick cooking spray. Combine turkey, egg and milk in large bowl; stir in bread crumbs, parsley and remaining ⅛ teaspoon pepper. Shape mixture into small balls; arrange on prepared baking sheet. Bake 25 minutes or until no longer pink in center.

3. Turn **CROCK-POT®** slow cooker to HIGH. Add meatballs to **CROCK-POT®** slow cooker. Cover; cook on HIGH 45 minutes to 1 hour or until meatballs are heated through. Remove and discard bay leaf. Prepare pasta according to package directions; drain. Place pasta in serving bowl; top with meatballs and sauce.

Makes 4 servings

Nutrition Information: Serving Size 1 cup pasta with ½ cup sauce and 6 meatballs, Calories 479, Total Fat 10g, Saturated Fat 3g, Protein 35g, Carbohydrate 65g, Cholesterol 119mg, Dietary Fiber 6g, Sodium 273mg

Vegetarian Main Dishes

Ziti Ratatouille

- **1 large eggplant, peeled and cut into 1/2-inch pieces (about 1 1/2 pounds)**
- **2 medium zucchini, cut into 1/2-inch pieces**
- **1 green or red bell pepper, cut into 1/2-inch pieces**
- **1 large yellow onion, chopped**
- **4 cloves garlic, minced**
- **1 jar (about 24 ounces) marinara sauce**
- **2 cans (about 14 ounces *each*) diced tomatoes with garlic and onions**
- **1 can (6 ounces) pitted black olives, drained**
- **1 package (8 ounces) uncooked ziti noodles**
- **Lemon juice (optional)**
- **Grated Parmesan cheese (optional)**

1. Combine eggplant, zucchini, bell pepper, onion, garlic, marinara sauce and tomatoes in **CROCK-POT®** slow cooker. Cover; cook on LOW 4 1/2 hours.

2. Stir in olives and pasta. Cover; cook on LOW 25 minutes. Drizzle with lemon juice and sprinkle with Parmesan cheese, if desired.

Makes 8 servings

Nutrition Information: Serving Size about 1 1/2 cups, Calories 275, Total Fat 7g, Saturated Fat 1g, Protein 8g, Carbohydrate 47g, Cholesterol 2mg, Dietary Fiber 7g, Sodium 692mg

Bean and Vegetable Burritos

2 **tablespoons chili powder**

2 **teaspoons dried oregano**

1½ **teaspoons ground cumin**

1 **large sweet potato, diced**

1 **can (about 15 ounces) black beans, rinsed and drained**

4 **cloves garlic, minced**

1 **medium yellow onion, halved and thinly sliced**

1 **jalapeño pepper, seeded and minced***

1 **green bell pepper, chopped**

1 **cup frozen corn, thawed and drained**

3 **tablespoons lime juice**

1 **tablespoon chopped fresh cilantro**

¾ **cup (3 ounces) shredded Monterey Jack cheese**

6 **(10-inch) flour tortillas, warmed**

Jalapeño peppers can sting and irritate the skin, so wear rubber gloves when handling peppers and do not touch your eyes.

1. Combine chili powder, oregano and cumin in small bowl. Layer ingredients in **CROCK-POT®** slow cooker in following order: sweet potato, beans, half of chili powder mixture, garlic, onion, jalapeño pepper, bell pepper, remaining half of chili powder mixture and corn. Cover; cook on LOW 5 hours or until sweet potato is tender. Stir in lime juice and cilantro.

2. Spoon 2 tablespoons cheese into center of each tortilla. Top with 1 cup filling. Fold up bottom edge of tortillas over filling; fold in sides and roll to enclose filling.

Makes 6 servings

Nutrition Information: Serving Size 1 burrito, Calories 392, Total Fat 11g, Saturated Fat 4g, Protein 14g, Carbohydrate 60g, Cholesterol 15mg, Dietary Fiber 8g, Sodium 800mg

Italian Escarole and White Bean Stew

1 tablespoon olive oil

1 medium yellow onion, chopped

3 medium carrots, cut into ½-inch-thick rounds

2 cloves garlic, minced

1 can (about 14 ounces) vegetable broth

1 head (about 12 ounces) escarole, base trimmed and cut into 1-inch-wide strips

2 cans (about 15 ounces *each*) Great Northern beans, rinsed and drained

¼ teaspoon red pepper flakes

Grated Parmesan cheese (optional)

Tip

Escarole is very leafy and easily fills a 4½-quart **CROCK-POT®** slow cooker when raw, but it shrinks dramatically as it cooks down. This recipe makes four portions, but can easily be doubled. Simply double the quantities of all the ingredients listed and be sure to use a 6-quart (or larger) **CROCK-POT®** slow cooker.

1. Heat oil in medium skillet over medium-high heat. Add onion and carrots; cook and stir 3 to 5 minutes or until onion is tender. Add garlic; cook and stir 1 minute or until fragrant. Remove to **CROCK-POT®** slow cooker. Pour in broth.

2. Wash escarole in large bowl of cold water. Lift out by handfuls, leaving sand or dirt in bottom of bowl. Shake to remove excess water, but do not dry. Add to vegetable mixture in **CROCK-POT®** slow cooker. Add beans and red pepper flakes.

3. Cover; cook on LOW 7 to 8 hours or on HIGH 3½ to 4 hours or until escarole is wilted and very tender. Sprinkle each serving evenly with Parmesan cheese, if desired.

Makes 4 servings

Nutrition Information: Serving Size about 1½ cups, Calories 336, Total Fat 5g, Saturated Fat 1g, Protein 18g, Carbohydrate 58g, Cholesterol 0mg, Dietary Fiber 15g, Sodium 474mg

Curried Potatoes, Cauliflower and Peas

1 **tablespoon vegetable oil**

1 **large yellow onion, chopped**

2 **tablespoons peeled and minced fresh ginger**

2 **cloves garlic, chopped**

2 **pounds red-skinned potatoes, cut into ½-inch-thick rounds**

1 **teaspoon garam masala***

1 **teaspoon salt**

1 **small head cauliflower (about 1¼ pounds), trimmed and broken into florets**

1 **cup vegetable broth**

2 **ripe plum tomatoes, seeded and chopped**

1 **cup frozen peas, thawed**

Hot cooked basmati or long grain rice (optional)

**Garam masala is an Indian spice blend available in the spice aisle of many supermarkets.
If garam masala is unavailable substitute ½ teaspoon ground cumin and ½ teaspoon ground
coriander seeds.*

1. Heat oil in large skillet over medium heat. Add onion, ginger and garlic; cook and stir until onion is tender. Remove from heat.

2. Put potatoes in **CROCK-POT**® slow cooker. Mix garam masala and salt in small bowl. Sprinkle half of spice mixture over potatoes. Top with onion mixture, then cauliflower. Sprinkle remaining spice mixture over cauliflower. Pour in broth. Cover; cook on HIGH 3½ hours.

3. Remove cover; gently stir in tomatoes and peas. Cover; cook on HIGH 30 minutes or until potatoes are tender. Serve over rice, if desired.

Makes 6 servings

Nutrition Information: Serving Size about 1 cup, Calories 174, Total Fat 3g, Saturated Fat 0g, Protein 6g, Carbohydrate 34g, Cholesterol 0mg, Dietary Fiber 5g, Sodium 569mg

Vegetarian Main Dishes

Black Bean and Mushroom Chilaquiles

  2 **tablespoons olive oil**

  1 **medium yellow onion, chopped**

  1 **medium green bell pepper, chopped**

  1 **jalapeño pepper, seeded and minced***

  2 **cans (about 15 ounces *each*) black beans, rinsed and drained**

  1 **can (about 14 ounces) diced tomatoes**

 10 **ounces white mushrooms, cut into quarters**

 1½ **teaspoons ground cumin**

 1½ **teaspoons dried oregano**

  1 **cup (4 ounces) shredded sharp white Cheddar cheese, plus additional for garnish**

  6 **cups baked corn tortilla chips**

*Jalapeño peppers can sting and irritate the skin, so wear rubber gloves when handling peppers and do not touch your eyes.

1. Heat oil in medium skillet over medium heat. Add onion, bell pepper and jalapeño pepper; cook and stir 3 to 5 minutes or until onion is tender. Remove to **CROCK-POT®** slow cooker. Add beans, tomatoes, mushrooms, cumin and oregano. Cover; cook on LOW 6 hours or on HIGH 3 hours.

2. Remove cover; sprinkle 1 cup Cheddar cheese over beans and mushrooms. Cover; cook on HIGH 15 minutes or until cheese is melted; stir to combine.

3. To serve, coarsely crush 1 cup tortilla chips into individual serving bowls. Top with evenly with black bean mixture. Garnish with additional cheese.

Makes 6 servings

Nutrition Information: Serving Size about 1½ cups, Calories 347, Total Fat 11g, Saturated Fat 3g, Protein 14g, Carbohydrate 49g, Cholesterol 10mg, Dietary Fiber 9g, Sodium 755mg

Bean Ragoût with Cilantro-Cornmeal Dumplings

2 cans (about **14** ounces *each*) diced tomatoes

1 can (about **15** ounces) no-salt-added pinto beans, rinsed and drained

1 can (about **15** ounces) no-salt-added black beans, rinsed and drained

1½ cups chopped red bell peppers

1 large yellow onion, chopped

2 small zucchini, sliced

½ cup chopped green bell pepper

½ cup chopped celery

1 poblano pepper, seeded and chopped*

3 tablespoons chili powder

2 cloves garlic, minced

2 teaspoons ground cumin

1 teaspoon dried oregano

¼ teaspoon salt

⅛ teaspoon black pepper

Cilantro-Cornmeal Dumplings (recipe follows)

Poblano peppers can sting and irritate the skin, so wear rubber gloves when handling peppers and do not touch your eyes.

1. Combine tomatoes, beans, red bell peppers, onion, zucchini, green bell pepper, celery, poblano pepper, chili powder, garlic, cumin, oregano, salt and black pepper in **CROCK-POT®** slow cooker; mix well. Cover; cook on LOW 7 to 8 hours.

2. Prepare Cilantro-Cornmeal Dumplings 1 hour before serving. Turn **CROCK-POT®** slow cooker to HIGH. Drop dumplings by level tablespoonfuls on top of ragoût. Cover; cook on HIGH 1 hour or until toothpick inserted into dumplings comes out clean.

Makes 6 servings

Nutrition Information: Serving Size about 2 cups ragoût and 3 dumplings, Calories 256, Total Fat 4g, Saturated Fat 1g, Protein 12g, Carbohydrate 44g, Cholesterol 2mg, Dietary Fiber 12g, Sodium 721mg

Bean Ragoût with Cilantro-Cornmeal Dumplings

Cilantro-Cornmeal Dumplings

- ¼ **cup all-purpose flour**
- ¼ **cup yellow cornmeal**
- ½ **teaspoon baking powder**
- ¼ **teaspoon salt**
- 1 **tablespoon shortening**
- 1 **tablespoon shredded Cheddar cheese**
- 2 **teaspoons minced fresh cilantro**
- ¼ **cup reduced-fat (2%) milk**

Combine flour, cornmeal, baking powder and salt in medium bowl; stir well. Cut in shortening with pastry blender or two knives until mixture resembles coarse crumbs. Stir in cheese and cilantro. Pour milk into flour mixture; stir just until dry ingredients are moistened.

Vegetable Curry

4 **baking potatoes, diced**

1 **large yellow onion, chopped**

1 **red bell pepper, chopped**

2 **carrots, diced**

2 **tomatoes, chopped**

1 **can (6 ounces) tomato paste**

¾ **cup water**

2 **teaspoons cumin seeds**

½ **teaspoon salt**

½ **teaspoon garlic powder**

3 **cups cauliflower florets**

1 **package (10 ounces) frozen peas, thawed**

Combine potatoes, onion, bell pepper, carrots and tomatoes in **CROCK-POT®** slow cooker. Stir in tomato paste, water, cumin seeds, salt and garlic powder. Add cauliflower; stir well. Cover; cook on LOW 8 to 9 hours or until vegetables are tender. Stir in peas just before serving.

Makes 6 servings

Nutrition Information: Serving Size about 1½ cups, Calories 191, Total Fat 1g, Saturated Fat 0g, Protein 7g, Carbohydrate 41g, Cholesterol 0mg, Dietary Fiber 9g, Sodium 464mg

Vegetarian Paella

- **2** teaspoons canola oil
- **1** cup chopped onion
- **2** cloves garlic, minced
- **1** cup uncooked brown rice
- **2¼** cups vegetable broth
- **1** can (about 14 ounces) no-salt-added stewed tomatoes
- **1** small zucchini, halved lengthwise and sliced into ½-inch thickness (about 1¼ cups)
- **1** cup coarsely chopped carrots
- **1** cup chopped red bell pepper
- **1** teaspoon Italian seasoning
- **½** teaspoon ground turmeric
- **⅛** teaspoon ground red pepper
- **1** can (about 14 ounces) quartered artichoke hearts, drained
- **½** cup frozen peas, thawed

1. Heat oil in large skillet over medium-high heat. Add onion; cook and stir 6 to 7 minutes or until tender. Stir in garlic.

2. Combine onion mixture and rice in **CROCK-POT**® slow cooker. Add broth, tomtatoes, zucchini, carrots, bell pepper, Italian seasoning, turmeric and ground red pepper; mix well. Cover; cook on LOW 4 hours or on HIGH 2 hours or until liquid is absorbed.

3. Stir in artichokes and peas. Cover; cook on LOW 5 to 10 minutes or until vegetables are tender.

Makes 6 servings

Nutrition Information: Serving Size about 1½ cups, Calories 241, Total Fat 7g, Saturated Fat 1g, Protein 5g, Carbohydrate 43g, Cholesterol 0mg, Dietary Fiber 7g, Sodium 470mg

Vegetarian Main Dishes

Caribbean Sweet Potato and Bean Stew

2 **medium sweet potatoes (about 1 pound), cut into 1-inch pieces**

2 **cups frozen cut green beans, thawed**

1 **can (about 15 ounces) black beans, rinsed and drained**

1 **can (about 14 ounces) reduced-sodium vegetable broth**

1 **small yellow onion, sliced**

2 **teaspoons Caribbean jerk seasoning**

½ **teaspoon dried thyme**

¼ **teaspoon salt**

¼ **teaspoon ground cinnamon**

⅓ **cup slivered almonds, toasted***

*To toast almonds, spread in single layer in heavy skillet. Cook and stir over medium heat 1 to 2 minutes or until nuts are lightly browned.

Combine sweet potatoes, beans, broth, onion, jerk seasoning, thyme, salt and cinnamon in **CROCK-POT®** slow cooker. Cover; cook on LOW 5 to 6 hours or until vegetables are tender. Sprinkle each serving evenly with almonds.

Makes 4 servings

Nutrition Information: Serving Size about 2 cups, Calories 221, Total Fat 5g, Saturated Fat 0g, Protein 9g, Carbohydrate 34g, Cholesterol 0mg, Dietary Fiber 9g, Sodium 708mg

Ratatouille with Chickpeas

- **3 tablespoons olive oil, divided**
- **4 cloves garlic, minced**
- **1 yellow onion, cut into ½-inch pieces**
  Salt and black pepper (optional)
- **4 small Italian eggplants, peeled and cut into ¾- to 1-inch pieces**
- **2 cups canned crushed tomatoes**
- **1 red bell pepper, cut into ¾- to 1-inch pieces**
- **1 yellow bell pepper, cut into ¾- to 1-inch pieces**
- **1 orange bell pepper, cut into ¾- to 1-inch pieces**
- **3 small zucchini, cut into ¾-inch pieces**
- **1 can (about 15 ounces) chickpeas, rinsed and drained**
- **¼ cup chopped fresh basil**
- **2 tablespoons chopped fresh thyme**
- **½ to 1 teaspoon red pepper flakes**
  Sprigs fresh basil (optional)

1. Heat 1 tablespoon oil in large skillet over medium-low heat. Add garlic and onion; cook and stir 2 to 3 minutes or until tender. Season eggplants with salt and black pepper, if desired. Add to skillet; cook and stir 1 to 2 minutes. Turn heat to low; cook 4 to 5 minutes or until eggplants are tender. Remove to **CROCK-POT®** slow cooker.

2. Stir in tomatoes, bell peppers, zucchini, chickpeas, remaining 2 tablespoons oil, chopped basil, thyme and red pepper flakes. Cover; cook on LOW 7 to 8 hours or on HIGH 4½ to 5 hours. Garnish with basil sprigs.

Makes 8 servings

Nutrition Information: Serving Size about 1½ cups, Calories 190, Total Fat 7g, Saturated Fat 1g, Protein 6g, Carbohydrate 29g, Cholesterol 0mg, Dietary Fiber 8g, Sodium 257mg

Vegetarian Main Dishes

Hearty Lentil Stew

1 **cup dried lentils, rinsed and sorted**

1 **package (16 ounces) frozen green beans, thawed**

2 **cups cauliflower florets**

1 **cup chopped yellow onion**

1 **cup baby carrots, cut into halves crosswise**

3 **cups fat-free reduced-sodium vegetable broth**

2 **teaspoons ground cumin**

¾ **teaspoon ground ginger**

1 **can (15 ounces) chunky tomato sauce with garlic and herbs**

½ **cup dry-roasted peanuts**

1. Place lentils in **CROCK-POT®** slow cooker. Top with beans, cauliflower, onion and carrots.

2. Combine broth, cumin and ginger in large bowl; mix well. Pour over vegetables in **CROCK-POT®** slow cooker. Cover; cook on LOW 9 to 11 hours.

3. Stir in tomato sauce. Cover; cook on LOW 10 minutes. Sprinkle each serving evenly with peanuts.

Makes 6 servings

Nutrition Information: Serving Size about 1½ cups, Calories 265, Total Fat 7g, Saturated Fat 1g, Protein 15g, Carbohydrate 39g, Cholesterol 0mg, Dietary Fiber 15g, Sodium 504mg

Spinach and Ricotta Stuffed Shells

18 uncooked jumbo pasta shells (about half of a 12-ounce package)

1 package (15 ounces) reduced-fat ricotta cheese

7 ounces frozen chopped spinach, thawed and squeezed dry

½ cup grated reduced-fat Parmesan cheese

1 egg, lightly beaten

1 clove garlic, minced

½ teaspoon salt

1 jar (26 ounces) marinara sauce

½ cup (2 ounces) shredded reduced-fat mozzarella cheese

1 teaspoon olive oil

1. Cook pasta shells according to package directions until almost tender. Drain well. Combine ricotta cheese, spinach, Parmesan cheese, egg, garlic and salt in medium bowl.

2. Pour ¼ cup marinara sauce in bottom of **CROCK-POT**® slow cooker. Spoon 2 to 3 tablespoons ricotta mixture into 1 pasta shell and place in bottom of **CROCK-POT**® slow cooker. Repeat with enough additional shells to cover bottom of **CROCK-POT**® slow cooker. Top with another ¼ cup marinara sauce. Repeat with remaining pasta shells and filling. Top with any remaining marinara sauce and sprinkle with mozzarella cheese. Drizzle with oil. Cover; cook on HIGH 3 to 4 hours or until mozzarella cheese is melted and sauce is heated through.

Makes 6 servings

Nutrition Information: Serving Size about 3 shells, Calories 385, Total Fat 8g, Saturated Fat 4g, Protein 18g, Carbohydrate 59g, Cholesterol 50mg, Dietary Fiber 5g, Sodium 727mg

Vegetarian Main Dishes

Southwestern Stuffed Peppers

4 green bell peppers

1 can (about 15 ounces) black beans, rinsed and drained

1 cup (4 ounces) shredded pepper jack cheese

¾ cup medium salsa

½ cup frozen corn, thawed

½ cup chopped green onions

⅓ cup uncooked long grain rice

1 teaspoon chili powder

½ teaspoon ground cumin

Sour cream (optional)

Variation

For firmer rice, substitute converted rice for regular long grain rice.

1. Cut thin slice off top of each bell pepper. Carefully remove seeds and membranes, leaving peppers whole.

2. Combine beans, cheese, salsa, corn, green onions, rice, chili powder and cumin in medium bowl. Spoon filling evenly into each pepper. Place peppers in **CROCK-POT®** slow cooker. Cover; cook on LOW 4 to 6 hours. Serve with sour cream, if desired.

Makes 4 servings

Nutrition Information: Serving Size 1 stuffed pepper, Calories 323, Total Fat 10g, Saturated Fat 3g, Protein 15g, Carbohydrate 43g, Cholesterol 30mg, Dietary Fiber 7g, Sodium 796mg

Vegetarian Sausage Rice

- **2 cups chopped green bell peppers**
- **1 can (about 15 ounces) no-salt-added dark kidney beans, rinsed and drained**
- **1 can (about 14 ounces) diced tomatoes with green bell peppers and onions**
- **1 cup chopped yellow onion**
- **1 cup sliced celery**
- **1 cup water, divided**
- **¾ cup uncooked converted long grain rice**
- **1¼ teaspoons salt**
- **1 teaspoon hot pepper sauce, plus additional for garnish**
- **½ teaspoon dried thyme**
- **½ teaspoon red pepper flakes**
- **3 whole bay leaves**
- **2 tablespoons extra virgin olive oil**
- **1 package (8 ounces) vegetable-protein breakfast patties, thawed and diced**
- **½ cup chopped fresh Italian parsley**

1. Combine bell peppers, beans, tomatoes, onion, celery, ½ cup water, rice, salt, 1 teaspoon hot pepper sauce, thyme, red pepper flakes and bay leaves in **CROCK-POT**® slow cooker. Cover; cook on LOW 4 to 5 hours. Remove and discard bay leaves.

2. Heat oil in large skillet over medium-high heat. Add breakfast patties; cook 2 minutes or until lightly browned. Remove to **CROCK-POT**® slow cooker. Do not stir.

3. Add remaining ½ cup water to skillet; bring to a boil over high heat. Boil 1 minute, stirring to scrape up any browned bits. Add liquid and parsley to **CROCK-POT**® slow cooker; stir gently to blend. Serve with additional hot pepper sauce, if desired.

Makes 8 servings

Nutrition Information: Serving Size about 1¼ cups, Calories 198, Total Fat 5g, Saturated Fat 1g, Protein 11g, Carbohydrate 30g, Cholesterol 0mg, Dietary Fiber 7g, Sodium 715mg

Vegetarian Main Dishes

Broccoli and Cheese Strata

2 cups chopped broccoli florets

4 slices firm white bread, ½ inch thick

1 tablespoon unsalted butter

1 cup (4 ounces) shredded Cheddar cheese

1½ cups low-fat (1%) milk

2 eggs

2 egg whites

½ teaspoon salt

½ teaspoon hot pepper sauce

⅛ teaspoon black pepper

1 cup water

1. Spray 1-quart casserole or soufflé dish that fits inside of 2½- to 3-quart **CROCK-POT®** slow cooker with nonstick cooking spray. Fill large saucepan with water; bring to a boil. Add broccoli; cook 5 minutes or until tender. Drain.

2. Spread one side of each bread slice with butter. Arrange 2 slices bread, buttered sides up, in prepared casserole dish. Layer cheese, broccoli and remaining 2 bread slices, buttered sides down. Whisk milk, eggs, egg whites, salt, hot pepper sauce and black pepper in medium bowl; slowly pour over bread.

3. Place small wire rack in **CROCK-POT®** slow cooker. Pour in 1 cup water. Place casserole on rack. Cover; cook on HIGH 3 hours.

Makes 4 servings

Nutrition Information: Serving Size ¼ strata, Calories 201, Total Fat 8g, Saturated Fat 4g, Protein 13g, Carbohydrate 20g, Cholesterol 91mg, Dietary Fiber 1g, Sodium 618mg

Corn Bread and Bean Casserole

Nonstick cooking spray
1 **medium yellow onion, chopped**
1 **medium green bell pepper, diced**
2 **cloves garlic, minced**
1 **can (about 15 ounces) no-salt-added red kidney beans, rinsed and drained**
1 **can (about 15 ounces) no-salt-added pinto beans, rinsed and drained**
1 **can (about 14 ounces) no-salt-added diced tomatoes**
1 **can (8 ounces) no-salt-added tomato sauce**
1 **teaspoon chili powder**
½ **teaspoon ground cumin**
½ **teaspoon black pepper**
¼ **teaspoon hot pepper sauce**
1 **cup yellow cornmeal**
1 **cup all-purpose flour**
2½ **teaspoons baking powder**
1 **tablespoon sugar**
½ **teaspoon salt**
1¼ **cups reduced-fat (2%) milk**
2 **eggs**
3 **tablespoons vegetable oil**
1 **can (8½ ounces) cream-style corn, undrained**

1. Coat inside of **CROCK-POT®** slow cooker with cooking spray. Spray medium skillet with cooking spray; heat over medium heat. Add onion, bell pepper and garlic; cook and stir 3 to 5 minutes or until vegetables are tender. Remove to **CROCK-POT®** slow cooker.

2. Stir in beans, tomatoes, tomato sauce, chili powder, cumin, black pepper and hot pepper sauce. Cover; cook on HIGH 1 hour.

3. Meanwhile, combine cornmeal, flour, baking powder, sugar and salt in large bowl. Combine milk, eggs and oil in small bowl; stir in corn. Add milk mixture to cornmeal mixture; stir just until combined. Spoon evenly over bean mixture in **CROCK-POT®** slow cooker. Cover; cook on HIGH 1½ to 2 hours or until corn bread topping is golden brown.

Makes 8 servings

Nutrition Information: Serving Size about 1½ cups, Calories 356, Total Fat 8g, Saturated Fat 1g, Protein 14g, Carbohydrate 58g, Cholesterol 57mg, Dietary Fiber 10g, Sodium 660mg

Slow-Cooked Summer Vegetable Stew

1 cup reduced-sodium vegetable broth

1 can (about 15 ounces) chickpeas, rinsed and drained

2 medium zucchini or summer squash, or combination, cut into 1/2-inch pieces

4 large plum tomatoes, cut into 1/2-inch pieces

1 cup frozen corn, thawed

1/2 to 1 teaspoon dried rosemary

1/4 cup grated Asiago or Parmesan cheese

1 tablespoon chopped fresh Italian parsley

Tip
Layer the ingredients in the order given to ensure they are all cooked properly.

Combine broth, chickpeas, zucchini, tomatoes, corn and rosemary in **CROCK-POT®** slow cooker; mix well. Cover; cook on LOW 8 hours or on HIGH 5 hours. Top each serving evenly with cheese and parsley.

Makes 4 servings

Nutrition Information: Serving Size 1¼ cups, Calories 168, Total Fat 3g, Saturated Fat 7g, Protein 9g, Carbohydrate 28g, Cholesterol 3mg, Dietary Fiber 6g, Sodium 317mg

Mediterranean Stew

- **2 pounds butternut squash, peeled and cut into 1-inch pieces**
- **2 cups unpeeled eggplant, cut into 1-inch pieces**
- **2 cups sliced zucchini**
- **1 can (about 15 ounces) chickpeas, rinsed and drained**
- **1 package (10 ounces) frozen cut okra, thawed**
- **1 can (8 ounces) tomato sauce**
- **1 cup chopped yellow onion**
- **1 medium tomato, chopped**
- **1 medium carrot, sliced**
- **½ cup vegetable broth**
- **⅓ cup raisins**
- **1 clove garlic, minced**
- **½ teaspoon ground cumin**
- **½ teaspoon ground turmeric**
- **¼ teaspoon ground red pepper**
- **¼ teaspoon ground cinnamon**
- **¼ teaspoon paprika**
- **Hot cooked couscous or rice (optional)**
- **Chopped fresh Italian parsley (optional)**

Combine squash, eggplant, zucchini, chickpeas, okra, tomato sauce, onion, tomato, carrot, broth, raisins, garlic, cumin, turmeric, ground red pepper, cinnamon and paprika in **CROCK-POT®** slow cooker; stir to blend. Cover; cook on LOW 8 to 10 hours. Serve over couscous, if desired. Garnished with parsley.

Makes 6 servings

Nutrition Information: Serving Size about 1¾ cups, Calories 389, Total Fat 2g, Saturated Fat 0g, Protein 13g, Carbohydrate 84g, Cholesterol 0mg, Dietary Fiber 12g, Sodium 470mg

Side Dishes

Braised Sweet and Sour Cabbage with Apples

- **2 tablespoons unsalted butter**
- **6 cups coarsely shredded red cabbage**
- **1 large sweet apple, peeled, cored and cut into bite-size pieces**
- **3 whole cloves**
- **½ cup raisins**
- **½ cup apple cider**
- **3 tablespoons cider vinegar, divided**
- **2 tablespoons packed dark brown sugar**
- **½ teaspoon salt**
- **¼ teaspoon black pepper**

1. Melt butter in large skillet over medium heat. Add cabbage; cook and stir 3 minutes or until cabbage is glossy. Remove to **CROCK-POT®** slow cooker.

2. Add apple, cloves, raisins, apple cider, 2 tablespoons vinegar, brown sugar, salt and pepper. Cover; cook on LOW 2½ to 3 hours. To serve, remove cloves and stir in remaining 1 tablespoon vinegar.

Makes 6 servings

Nutrition Information: Serving Size about 1¼ cups, Calories 153, Total Fat 4g, Saturated Fat 2g, Protein 2g, Carbohydrate 29g, Cholesterol 10mg, Dietary Fiber 3g, Sodium 227mg

Side Dishes

Wild Rice with Fruit and Nuts

> **5** **cups 99% fat-free reduced-sodium chicken broth**
>
> **2** **cups uncooked wild rice, rinsed***
>
> **1** **cup orange juice**
>
> **½** **cup dried cranberries**
>
> **½** **cup chopped raisins**
>
> **½** **cup chopped dried apricots**
>
> **½** **cup slivered almonds, toasted****
>
> **2** **tablespoons unsalted butter, melted**
>
> **1** **teaspoon ground cumin**
>
> **2** **green onions, thinly sliced**
>
> **2** **tablespoons chopped fresh parsley**

*Do not use parboiled rice or a blend containing parboiled rice.

**To toast almonds, spread in single layer in small skillet. Cook and stir over medium heat 1 to 2 minutes or until nuts are lightly browned.

1. Combine broth, rice, orange juice, cranberries, raisins, apricots, almonds, butter and cumin in **CROCK-POT®** slow cooker; stir to blend.

2. Cover; cook on LOW 7 hours or on HIGH 2½ to 3 hours, stirring halfway through cooking time. Add green onions and parsley. Cover; cook on LOW 10 minutes.

Makes 8 servings

Nutrition Information: Serving Size about ¾ cup, Calories 301, Total Fat 7g, Saturated Fat 2g, Protein 8g, Carbohydrate 54g, Cholesterol 8mg, Dietary Fiber 4g, Sodium 586mg

Side Dishes

Skinny Corn Bread

- 1¼ cups all-purpose flour
- ¾ cup yellow cornmeal
- ¼ cup sugar
- 1 teaspoon baking powder
- 1 teaspoon baking soda
- ¼ teaspoon seasoned salt
- 1 cup fat-free buttermilk
- ¼ cup cholesterol-free egg substitute
- ¼ cup canola oil

Tip
This recipe works best in round **CROCK-POT®** slow cookers.

1. Coat inside of 3-quart **CROCK-POT®** slow cooker with nonstick cooking spray.

2. Combine flour, cornmeal, sugar, baking powder, baking soda and seasoned salt in large bowl. Make well in center of dry mixture. Pour buttermilk, egg substitute and oil in well; stir just until moistened. Pour mixture into **CROCK-POT®** slow cooker.

3. Cover; cook on LOW 3 to 4 hours or on HIGH 45 minutes to 1½ hours or until edge is golden and knife inserted into center comes out clean. Remove stoneware from **CROCK-POT®** slow cooker. Cool on wire rack 10 minutes. Remove bread from stoneware; cool completely.

Makes 8 servings

Nutrition Information: Serving Size ⅛ of loaf, Calories 228, Total Fat 8g, Saturated Fat 1g, Protein 5g, Carbohydrate 35g, Cholesterol 1mg, Dietary Fiber 1g, Sodium 300mg

Wild Rice and Dried Cherry Risotto

1 cup lightly salted dry-roasted peanuts

2 tablespoons sesame oil, divided

1 cup chopped yellow onion

1 cup diced carrots

1 cup chopped green or red bell pepper

6 ounces uncooked wild rice

½ cup dried cherries

⅛ teaspoon red pepper flakes

4 cups hot water

¼ cup reduced-sodium soy sauce

½ teaspoon salt

1. Coat inside of **CROCK-POT®** slow cooker with nonstick cooking spray. Heat large skillet over medium-high heat. Add peanuts; cook and stir 2 to 3 minutes or until nuts begin to brown. Remove nuts to plate; set aside.

2. Heat 2 teaspoons oil in same skillet over medium-high heat. Add onion; cook and stir 6 minutes or until richly browned. Remove to **CROCK-POT®** slow cooker.

3. Stir carrots, bell pepper, rice, cherries and red pepper flakes into **CROCK-POT®** slow cooker. Stir in water. Cover; cook on HIGH 3 hours.

4. Turn off heat. Let stand 15 minutes, uncovered, until rice absorbs liquid. Stir in soy sauce, peanuts, remaining 4 teaspoons oil and salt.

Makes 10 servings

Nutrition Information: Serving Size about ¾ cup, Calories 202, Total Fat 9g, Saturated Fat 1g, Protein 7g, Carbohydrate 24g, Cholesterol 0mg, Dietary Fiber 3g, Sodium 282mg

Cuban Black Beans and Rice

3¾ cups 99% fat-free reduced-sodium chicken broth

1½ cups uncooked brown rice

1 large yellow onion, chopped

1 jalapeño pepper, seeded and chopped*

3 cloves garlic, minced

2 teaspoons ground cumin

1 teaspoon salt

2 cans (about 15 ounces *each*) fat-free no-salt-added black beans, rinsed and drained

1 tablespoon lime juice

Sour cream (optional)

Chopped green onions (optional)

*Jalapeño peppers can sting and irritate the skin, so wear rubber gloves when handling peppers and do not touch your eyes.

1. Combine broth, rice, onion, jalapeño pepper, garlic, cumin and salt in **CROCK-POT®** slow cooker. Cover; cook on LOW 7½ hours or until rice is tender.

2. Stir in beans and lime juice. Cover; cook on LOW 15 to 20 minutes or until beans are heated through. Top with sour cream and green onions, if desired.

Makes 6 servings

Nutrition Information: Serving Size about 1 cup, Calories 300, Total Fat 2g, Saturated Fat 0g, Protein 12g, Carbohydrate 59g, Cholesterol 0mg, Dietary Fiber 9g, Sodium 303mg

Side Dishes

Southwestern Corn and Beans

- **1 tablespoon olive oil**
- **1 large onion, diced**
- **1 jalapeño pepper, diced***
- **1 clove garlic, minced**
- **2 cans (15 ounces each) no-salt-added light red kidney beans, rinsed and drained**
- **1 bag (16 ounces) frozen corn, thawed**
- **1 can (14½ ounces) no-salt-added diced tomatoes, undrained**
- **1 green bell pepper, cut into 1-inch pieces**
- **2 teaspoons medium-hot chili powder**
- **½ teaspoon salt**
- **½ teaspoon ground cumin**
- **½ teaspoon black pepper**
- **Sour cream or plain yogurt (optional)**
- **Sliced black olives (optional)**

***Jalapeño peppers can sting and irritate the skin, so wear rubber gloves when handling peppers and do not touch your eyes. Wash hands after handling.**

Tip

For a party, spoon this colorful vegetarian dish into hollowed-out bell peppers or bread bowls.

1. Heat oil in medium skillet over medium heat. Add onion, jalapeño pepper and garlic; cook 5 minutes. Combine onion mixture, beans, corn, tomatoes with juice, bell pepper, chili powder, salt, cumin and black pepper in **CROCK-POT®** slow cooker; mix well. Cover; cook on LOW 7 to 8 hours or on HIGH 2 to 3 hours.

2. Serve with sour cream and black olives, if desired.

Makes 6 servings

Nutrition Information: Serving Size about 1¼ cups, Calories 230, Total Fat 3g, Saturated Fat 1g, Protein 12g, Carbohydrate 40g, Cholesterol 0mg, Dietary Fiber 15g, Sodium 276mg

Side Dishes

Coconut-Lime Sweet Potatoes with Walnuts

2½ **pounds sweet potatoes, cut into 1-inch pieces**

8 **ounces shredded carrots**

¾ **cup reduced-fat shredded coconut, divided**

1 **tablespoon unsalted butter, melted**

3 **tablespoons sugar**

½ **teaspoon salt**

⅓ **cup walnuts, toasted, coarsely chopped and divided***

2 **teaspoons grated lime peel**

****To toast walnuts, spread in single layer in small skillet. Cook and stir over medium heat 1 to
2 minutes or until nuts are lightly browned.***

1. Combine sweet potatoes, carrots, ½ cup coconut, butter, sugar and salt in **CROCK-POT®** slow cooker. Cover; cook on LOW 5 to 6 hours or until sweet potatoes are tender.

2. Meanwhile, add remaining ¼ cup coconut into preheated small nonstick skillet; cook 4 minutes or until coconut is lightly browned. Remove to small bowl; cool completely.

3. Mash sweet potatoes. Stir in 3 tablespoons walnuts and lime peel. Sprinkle top of mashed sweet potatoes evenly with remaining walnuts and toasted coconut.

Makes 8 servings

Nutrition Information: Serving Size about ¾ cup, Calories 207, Total Fat 6g, Saturated Fat 2g, Protein 3g, Carbohydrate 37g, Cholesterol 4mg, Dietary Fiber 6g, Sodium 243mg

Side Dishes

Lemon Dilled Parsnips and Turnips

- **4 turnips, peeled and cut into ½-inch pieces**
- **3 parsnips, cut into ½-inch pieces**
- **2 cups 99% fat-free chicken broth**
- **¼ cup dried dill**
- **¼ cup chopped green onions**
- **¼ cup lemon juice**
- **1 teaspoon minced garlic**
- **¼ cup cold water**
- **¼ cup cornstarch**

1. Combine turnips, parsnips, broth, dill, green onions, lemon juice and garlic in **CROCK-POT®** slow cooker; stir until well blended. Cover; cook on LOW 3 to 4 hours or on HIGH 1 to 3 hours.

2. Stir water into cornstarch in small bowl until smooth. Whisk into **CROCK-POT®** slow cooker. Cover; cook on HIGH 15 minutes or until thickened.

Makes 10 servings

Nutrition Information: Serving Size about ³⁄₄ cup, Calories 70, Total Fat 0g, Saturated Fat 0g, Protein 2g, Carbohydrate 16g, Cholesterol 0mg, Dietary Fiber 3g, Sodium 226mg

Mexican-Style Spinach

3 packages (10 ounces *each*) frozen chopped spinach, thawed

1 tablespoon canola oil

1 onion, chopped

1 clove garlic, minced

2 Anaheim chiles, roasted, peeled and minced*

3 fresh tomatillos, roasted, husks removed and chopped**

6 tablespoons fat-free sour cream (optional)

To roast Anaheim chiles, heat large heavy skillet over medium-high heat. Add chiles; cook and turn until blackened all over. Place chiles in brown paper bag for 2 to 5 minutes. Remove chiles from bag; scrape off charred skin. Cut off top and pull out core. Slice lengthwise; scrape off veins and any remaining seeds with a knife.

**To roast tomatillos, heat large heavy skillet over medium heat. Add tomatillos with papery husks 10 minutes or until husks are brown and interior flesh is soft. Remove and discard husks when cool enough to handle.*

1. Place spinach in **CROCK-POT**® slow cooker.

2. Heat oil in large skillet over medium heat. Add onion and garlic; cook and stir 5 minutes or until onion is tender. Add chiles and tomatillos; cook 3 to 4 minutes. Remove onion mixture to **CROCK-POT**® slow cooker.

3. Cover; cook on LOW 4 to 6 hours. Serve with dollops of sour cream, if desired.

Makes 6 servings

Nutrition Information: Serving Size about ¾ cup, Calories 81, Total Fat 3g, Saturated Fat 0g, Protein 6g, Carbohydrate 10g, Cholesterol 0mg, Dietary Fiber 5g, Sodium 107mg

Side Dishes

Easy Dirty Rice

- ½ **pound reduced-fat Italian sausage**
- 2 **cups water**
- 1 **cup uncooked long grain rice**
- 1 **large yellow onion, finely chopped**
- 1 **large green bell pepper, finely chopped**
- ½ **cup finely chopped celery**
- ¼ **teaspoon salt**
- ½ **teaspoon ground red pepper**
- ½ **cup chopped fresh Italian parsley**

Tip
Try substituting brown rice for the white rice in this recipe. Since it contains the bran and the germ, it is more nutritious than ordinary white rice.

1. Brown sausage in skillet 6 to 8 minutes over medium-high heat, stirring to break up meat. Remove to **CROCK-POT®** slow cooker using slotted spoon.

2. Stir in water, rice, onion, bell pepper, celery, salt and ground red pepper. Cover; cook on LOW 2 hours. Stir in parsley.

Makes 4 servings

Nutrition Information: Serving Size about ¾ cup, Calories 192, Total Fat 5g, Saturated Fat 2g, Protein 7g, Carbohydrate 29g, Cholesterol 18mg, Dietary Fiber 2g, Sodium 273mg

Side Dishes

Parmesan Potato Wedges

   2 **pounds red potatoes, cut into ½-inch wedges**
  ¼ **cup finely chopped yellow onion**
1½ **teaspoons dried oregano**
  ½ **teaspoon salt**
  ¼ **teaspoon black pepper**
  2 **tablespoons butter, cubed**
  ¼ **cup (1 ounce) grated Parmesan cheese**

Layer potatoes, onion, oregano, salt, pepper and butter in **CROCK-POT®** slow cooker. Cover; cook on HIGH 4 hours. Remove potatoes to serving platter; sprinkle with cheese.

Makes 6 servings

Nutrition Information: Serving Size about ³⁄₄ cup, Calories 160, Total Fat 5g, Saturated Fat 3g, Protein 5g, Carbohydrate 25g, Cholesterol 14mg, Dietary Fiber 3g, Sodium 269mg

Lentils with Walnuts

1 **cup dried brown lentils, rinsed and sorted**
1 **small yellow onion, chopped**
1 **stalk celery, trimmed and chopped**
1 **large carrot, chopped**
¼ **teaspoon dried thyme**
3 **cups fat-free reduced-sodium chicken broth**
  Salt and black pepper (optional)
¼ **cup chopped walnuts**

1. Combine lentils, onion, celery, carrot, thyme and broth in **CROCK-POT®** slow cooker. Cover; cook on HIGH 3 hours. Do not overcook. (Lentils should absorb most or all of broth. Slightly tilt **CROCK-POT®** slow cooker to check.)

2. Season with salt and pepper, if desired. Spoon lentils into serving bowls. Sprinkle each serving evenly with walnuts.

Makes 6 servings

Nutrition Information: Serving Size ³⁄₄ cup, Calories 158, Total Fat 4g, Saturated Fat 0g, Protein 10g, Carbohydrate 22g, Cholesterol 0mg, Dietary Fiber 10g, Sodium 241mg

Parmesan Potato Wedges

Side Dishes

Orange-Spice Glazed Carrots

1 package (32 ounces) baby carrots

½ cup packed light brown sugar

½ cup orange juice

1 tablespoon unsalted butter

¾ teaspoon ground cinnamon

¼ teaspoon ground nutmeg

¼ cup cold water

2 tablespoons cornstarch

1. Combine carrots, brown sugar, orange juice, butter, cinnamon and nutmeg in **CROCK-POT®** slow cooker. Cover; cook on LOW 3½ to 4 hours or until carrots are crisp-tender. Spoon carrots into serving bowl.

2. Turn **CROCK-POT®** slow cooker to HIGH. Stir water into cornstarch in small bowl until smooth. Whisk into **CROCK-POT®** slow cooker. Cover; cook on HIGH 15 minutes or until thickened. Spoon sauce evenly over carrots.

Makes 6 servings

Nutrition Information: Serving Size about ¾ cup, Calories 179, Total Fat 2g, Saturated Fat 1g, Protein 2g, Carbohydrate 39g, Cholesterol 5mg, Dietary Fiber 4g, Sodium 6mg

Herbed Fall Vegetables

2 **medium Yukon Gold potatoes, cut into ½-inch pieces**

2 **medium sweet potatoes, cut into ½-inch pieces**

3 **parsnips, cut into ½-inch pieces**

1 **medium head of fennel, sliced and cut into ½-inch pieces**

1 **cup fat-free reduced-sodium chicken broth**

¾ **cup chopped fresh Italian parsley**

2 **tablespoons unsalted butter, cubed**

1 **tablespoon salt**

Black pepper (optional)

Combine potatoes, parsnips, fennel, broth, parsley butter and salt in **CROCK-POT®** slow cooker. Season with pepper, if desired. Cover; cook on LOW 4½ hours or on HIGH 3 hours, stirring halfway through cooking time.

Makes 6 servings

Nutrition Information: Serving Size about 1 cup, Calories 135, Total Fat 3g, Saturated Fat 2g, Protein 3g, Carbohydrate 26g, Cholesterol 8mg, Dietary Fiber 6g, Sodium 244mg

Side Dishes

Winter Squash and Apples

- **1 butternut squash (about 2 pounds), peeled, seeded and cut into 2-inch pieces**
- **2 apples, cored and cut into slices**
- **1 medium yellow onion, quartered and sliced**
- **¾ teaspoon salt**
- **½ teaspoon black pepper**
- **1½ tablespoons unsalted butter**

Place squash, apples, onion, salt and pepper in **CROCK-POT®** slow cooker; stir well. Cover; cook on LOW 6 to 7 hours or until vegetables are tender. Just before serving, stir in butter until melted.

Makes 6 servings

Nutrition Information: Serving Size about ¾ cup, Calories 133, Total Fat 3g, Saturated Fat 2g, Protein 2g, Carbohydrate 28g, Cholesterol 8mg, Dietary Fiber 5g, Sodium 299mg

Barley with Currants and Pine Nuts

1½ **teaspoons unsalted butter**

  1 **small onion, finely chopped**

  2 **cups fat-free reduced-sodium chicken broth**

 ½ **cup uncooked pearl barley**

 ½ **teaspoon salt**

 ¼ **teaspoon black pepper**

 ⅓ **cup currants**

 ¼ **cup pine nuts**

Melt butter in small skillet over medium-high heat. Add onion; cook and stir 2 minutes or until lightly browned. Remove to **CROCK-POT®** slow cooker. Add broth, barley, salt and pepper to **CROCK-POT®** slow cooker. Stir in currants. Cover; cook on LOW 3 hours. Stir in pine nuts just before serving.

Makes 4 servings

Nutrition Information: Serving Size about ½ cup, Calories 197, Total Fat 8g, Saturated Fat 1g, Protein 5g, Carbohydrate 30g, Cholesterol 4mg, Dietary Fiber 5g, Sodium 228mg

Side Dishes

Orange-Spiced Sweet Potatoes

2 pounds sweet potatoes, diced

½ cup packed dark brown sugar

Juice of 1 medium orange

2 tablespoons unsalted butter, cubed

1 teaspoon ground cinnamon

1 teaspoon vanilla

½ teaspoon ground nutmeg

½ teaspoon grated orange peel

¼ teaspoon salt

Chopped toasted pecans (optional)*

*To toast pecans, spread in single layer in small skillet. Cook and stir over medium heat 1 to 2 minutes or until nuts are lightly browned.

Tip

For a creamy texture, mash the potatoes with a potato masher or electric mixer. Add ¼ cup milk or whipping cream. Sprinkle with cinnamon-sugar and toasted pecans, if desired.

Place sweet potatoes, brown sugar, orange juice, butter, cinnamon, vanilla, nutmeg, orange peel and salt in **CROCK-POT®** slow cooker. Cover; cook on LOW 4 hours or on HIGH 2 hours. Sprinkle each serving with pecans, if desired.

Makes 8 servings

Nutrition Information: Serving Size about ¾ cup, Calories 198, Total Fat 5g, Saturated Fat 2g, Protein 2g, Carbohydrate 38g, Cholesterol 8mg, Dietary Fiber 4g, Sodium 140mg

Red Cabbage and Apples

- **1 small head red cabbage, cored and thinly sliced**
- **1 large apple, peeled and grated**
- **¾ cup sugar**
- **½ cup red wine vinegar**
- **1 teaspoon ground cloves**
- **½ cup bacon, crisp-cooked and crumbled (optional)**
- **Fresh apple slices (optional)**

Combine cabbage, grated apples, sugar, vinegar and cloves in **CROCK-POT®** slow cooker. Cover; cook on HIGH 6 hours, stirring halfway through cooking time. Sprinkle with bacon, if desired. Garnish with apple slices.

Makes 6 servings

Nutrition Information: Serving Size about ¾ cup, Calories 147, Total Fat 0g, Saturated Fat 0g, Protein 1g, Carbohydrate 37g, Cholesterol 0mg, Dietary Fiber 3g, Sodium 29mg

Side Dishes

Garlic and Herb Polenta

8 cups water

2 cups yellow cornmeal

2 teaspoons finely minced garlic

2 teaspoons salt

1 tablespoon unsalted butter, divided

3 tablespoons chopped fresh herbs such as parsley, chives, thyme or chervil (or a combination of any of these)

Tip
Polenta may also be poured into a greased pan and allowed to cool until set. Cut into squares or slice as desired to serve. For more added flavor, chill polenta slices until firm. Then grill or fry until golden brown.

Coat inside of **CROCK-POT®** slow cooker with nonstick cooking spray. Add water, cornmeal, garlic, salt and butter; stir. Cover; cook on LOW 4 hours or on HIGH 3 hours, stirring halfway through cooking time. Stir in chopped herbs just before serving.

Makes 6 servings

Nutrition Information: Serving Size about ²/₃ cup, Calories 168, Total Fat 2g, Saturated Fat 1g, Protein 3g, Carbohydrate 32g, Cholesterol 4mg, Dietary Fiber 2g, Sodium 303mg

Rustic Cheddar Mashed Potatoes

2 pounds russet potatoes, diced

1 cup water

2 tablespoons unsalted butter, cubed

¾ cup fat-free (skim) milk

¾ teaspoon salt

½ teaspoon black pepper

½ cup finely chopped green onions

2 tablespoons reduced-fat shredded Cheddar cheese

1. Combine potatoes, water and butter in **CROCK-POT®** slow cooker. Cover; cook on LOW 6 hours or on HIGH 3 hours. Remove potatoes to large bowl.

2. Beat potatoes with electric mixer at medium speed 2 to 3 minutes or until well blended. Add milk, salt and pepper; beat 2 minutes or until well blended.

3. Stir in green onions and cheese. Cover; let stand 15 minutes or until cheese is melted.

Makes 8 servings

Nutrition Information: Serving Size about ¾ cup, Calories 127, Total Fat 3g, Saturated Fat 2g, Protein 3g, Carbohydrate 22g, Cholesterol 10mg, Dietary Fiber 2g, Sodium 246mg

Spinach Gorgonzola Corn Bread

- **2 boxes (8½ ounces *each*) corn bread mix**
- **3 eggs**
- **½ cup fat-free half-and-half**
- **1 box (10 ounces) frozen chopped spinach, thawed and drained**
- **½ cup crumbled Gorgonzola**
- **1 teaspoon black pepper**
- **Paprika (optional)**

Note
Cook only on HIGH setting for proper crust and texture.

1. Coat inside of 4½-quart **CROCK-POT®** slow cooker with nonstick cooking spray.

2. Mix bread mix, eggs, half-and-half, spinach, Gorgonzola and pepper in medium bowl. Pour batter into **CROCK-POT®** slow cooker. Cover; cook on HIGH 1½ hours.

3. Remove stoneware to wire rack; cool completely. Invert onto large serving platter. Sprinkle with paprika, if desired.

Makes 12 servings

Nutrition Information: Serving Size 1 slice (¹/₁₂ loaf), Calories 134, Total Fat 4g, Saturated Fat 2g, Protein 9g, Carbohydrate 15g, Cholesterol 61mg, Dietary Fiber 3g, Sodium 251mg

Risi Bisi

1½ **cups uncooked converted long grain rice**

¾ **cup chopped yellow onion**

2 **cloves garlic, minced**

2 **cans (about 14 ounces *each*) reduced-sodium chicken broth**

⅓ **cup water**

¾ **teaspoon Italian seasoning**

½ **teaspoon dried basil**

½ **cup frozen peas, thawed**

¼ **cup grated Parmesan cheese**

¼ **cup toasted pine nuts (optional)***

***To toast pine nuts, spread in single layer in small skillet. Cook and stir over medium heat 1 to 2 minutes or until nuts are lightly browned.**

1. Combine rice, onion and garlic in **CROCK-POT**® slow cooker.

2. Bring broth and water to a boil over high heat in small saucepan. Stir broth mixture, Italian seasoning and basil into rice mixture in **CROCK-POT**® slow cooker. Cover; cook on LOW 2 to 3 hours or until liquid is absorbed.

3. Add peas. Cover; cook on LOW 1 hour. Stir in cheese. Sprinkle with pine nuts, if desired.

Makes 6 servings

Nutrition Information: Serving Size about ½ cup, Calories 158, Total Fat 1g, Saturated Fat 1g, Protein 5g, Carbohydrate 31g, Cholesterol 2mg, Dietary Fiber 1g, Sodium 279mg

Pesto Rice and Beans

1 can (about 15 ounces) no-salt-added Great Northern beans, rinsed and drained

1 can (about 14 ounces) fat-free reduced-sodium chicken broth

¾ cup uncooked converted long grain rice

1½ cups frozen cut green beans, thawed and drained

½ cup prepared pesto

Grated Parmesan cheese (optional)

Tip

Choose converted long grain rice, Arborio rice or wild rice for best results. Long, slow cooking can turn other types of rice into mush. If you prefer to use another type of rice instead of converted, cook it on the stove-top and add it to the **CROCK-POT®** slow cooker during the last 15 minutes of cooking.

1. Combine Great Northern beans, broth and rice in **CROCK-POT®** slow cooker. Cover; cook on LOW 2 hours.

2. Stir in green beans. Cover; cook on LOW 1 hour or until rice and beans are tender.

3. Turn off heat. Stir in pesto and Parmesan cheese, if desired. Let stand, covered, 5 minutes or until cheese is melted.

Makes 8 servings

Nutrition Information: Serving Size ½ cup, Calories 195, Total Fat 8g, Saturated Fat 2g, Protein 7g, Carbohydrate 24g, Cholesterol 5mg, Dietary Fiber 5g, Sodium 245mg

Greek Rice

2 **tablespoons unsalted butter**

1¾ **cups uncooked converted long grain rice**

2 **cans (14 ounces *each*) fat-free reduced-sodium chicken broth**

1 **teaspoon Greek seasoning**

1 **teaspoon ground oregano**

1 **cup pitted kalamata olives, drained and chopped**

¾ **cup chopped roasted red peppers**

Crumbled feta cheese (optional)

Chopped fresh Italian parsley (optional)

Melt butter in large skillet over medium-high heat. Add rice; cook and stir 4 minutes or until golden brown. Remove to **CROCK-POT®** slow cooker. Stir in broth, Greek seasoning and oregano. Cover; cook on LOW 4 hours or until liquid is absorbed. Stir in olives and red peppers. Cover; cook on LOW 5 minutes. Garnish with feta and parsley.

Makes 8 servings

Nutrition Information: Serving Size ¾ cup, Calories 175, Total Fat 4g, Saturated Fat 2g, Protein 3g, Carbohydrate 32g, Cholesterol 8mg, Dietary Fiber 0g, Sodium 297mg

Spiced Sweet Potatoes

2 **pounds sweet potatoes, cut into ¹/₂-inch pieces**

¹/₄ **cup packed dark brown sugar**

1 **teaspoon ground cinnamon**

¹/₂ **teaspoon ground nutmeg**

¹/₈ **teaspoon salt**

2 **tablespoons unsalted butter, cubed**

1 **teaspoon vanilla**

Combine sweet potatoes, brown sugar, cinnamon, nutmeg and salt in **CROCK-POT®** slow cooker; stir to blend. Cover; cook on LOW 7 hours or on HIGH 4 hours. Add butter and vanilla; stir to blend.

Makes 4 servings

Nutrition Information: Serving Size about 1 cup, Calories 258, Total Fat 3g, Saturated Fat 2g, Protein 4g, Carbohydrate 8g, Cholesterol 8mg, Dietary Fiber 7g, Sodium 196mg

Green Bean Casserole

2 packages (10 ounces *each*) frozen green beans, thawed

1 can (10¾ ounces) reduced-sodium condensed cream of mushroom soup, undiluted

1 tablespoon chopped parsley

1 tablespoon chopped roasted red peppers

1 teaspoon dried sage

½ teaspoon salt

½ teaspoon black pepper

¼ teaspoon ground nutmeg

½ cup toasted slivered almonds*

*To toast almonds, spread in single layer in small skillet. Cook and stir over medium heat 1 to 2 minutes or until nuts are lightly browned.

Combine green beans, soup, parsley, red pepper, sage, salt, black pepper and nutmeg in **CROCK-POT®** slow cooker. Cover; cook on LOW 3 to 4 hours. Sprinkle each serving evenly with almonds.

Makes 6 servings

Nutrition Information: Serving Size about ¾ cup, Calories 91, Total Fat 7g, Saturated Fat 1g, Protein 4g, Carbohydrate 13g, Cholesterol 2mg, Dietary Fiber 4g, Sodium 221mg

Desserts

Five-Spice Apple Crisp

1 **tablespoon unsalted butter, melted**

6 **Golden Delicious apples, peeled, cored and cut into ½-inch-thick slices**

¼ **cup packed light brown sugar**

2 **teaspoons lemon juice**

¾ **teaspoon Chinese five-spice powder or ½ teaspoon ground cinnamon and ¼ teaspoon ground allspice***

1 **cup coarsely crushed almond biscotti**

Whipped cream (optional)

Ground nutmeg (optional)

***Chinese five-spice powder is a blend of cinnamon, cloves, fennel seed, anise and Szechuan peppercorns. It is available in most supermarkets and at Asian grocery stores.**

Coat inside of 4½-quart **CROCK-POT®** slow cooker with butter. Add apples, brown sugar, lemon juice and five-spice powder; toss to combine. Cover; cook on LOW 3½ hours or until apples are tender. Sprinkle with cookies. Spoon evenly into bowls. Garnish with whipped cream and nutmeg.

Makes 6 servings

Nutrition Information: Serving Size ⅙ crisp, Calories 211, Total Fat 4g, Saturated Fat 2g, Protein 2g, Carbohydrate 44g, Cholesterol 5mg, Dietary Fiber 4g, Sodium 50mg

Desserts

English Bread Pudding

16 slices day-old, firm-textured white bread
 (1 small loaf), torn into 1- to 2-inch pieces

1¾ cups fat-free (skim) milk

1 package (8 ounces) mixed dried fruit, cut
 into small pieces

1 medium apple, cored and chopped

¼ cup chopped walnuts

⅓ cup packed brown sugar

2 tablespoons unsalted butter, melted

1 egg, lightly beaten

1 teaspoon ground cinnamon

¼ teaspoon ground nutmeg

¼ teaspoon ground cloves

Note

To make chopping dried fruits easier, cut fruit with kitchen scissors or chef's knife sprayed with nonstick cooking spray to prevent sticking.

1. Place bread in **CROCK-POT®** slow cooker. Pour milk over bread; let soak 30 minutes.

2. Stir in dried fruit, apple and walnuts. Combine brown sugar, butter, egg, cinnamon, nutmeg and cloves in small bowl; pour over bread mixture. Stir well to blend. Cover; cook on LOW 3½ to 4 hours or until toothpick inserted into center of pudding comes out clean.

Makes 8 servings

Nutrition Information: Serving Size about 1 cup, Calories 264, Total Fat 7g, Saturated Fat 2g, Protein 6g, Carbohydrate 49g, Cholesterol 28mg, Dietary Fiber 3g, Sodium 245mg

Desserts

Poached Autumn Fruits with Vanilla-Citrus Broth

2 Granny Smith apples, peeled, cored and halved (reserve cores)

2 Bartlett pears, peeled, cored and halved (reserve cores)

1 orange, peeled and halved

⅓ cup sugar

¼ cup plus 1 tablespoon honey

1 vanilla bean, split and seeded (reserve seeds)

1 cinnamon stick

Dried cranberries (optional)

Vanilla ice cream (optional)

1. Place apple and pear cores in **CROCK-POT®** slow cooker. Squeeze juice from orange halves into **CROCK-POT®** slow cooker. Add orange halves, sugar, honey, vanilla bean and seeds and cinnamon stick. Add apples, pears and enough water to cover fruit; stir to combine. Cover; cook on HIGH 2 hours or until fruit is tender.

2. Remove apple and pear halves; dice. Strain cooking liquid; discard solids. Return fruit and liquid to **CROCK-POT®** slow cooker. Stir in cranberries, if desired. Cover; cook on HIGH 10 to 15 minutes or until thickened. To serve, spoon fruit with sauce evenly into bowls. Top with vanilla ice cream, if desired.

Makes 6 servings

Nutrition Information: Serving Size about ¾ cup fruit and broth, Calories 175, Total Fat 0g, Saturated Fat 0g, Protein 1g, Carbohydrate 46g, Cholesterol 0mg, Dietary Fiber 4g, Sodium 2mg

Desserts

Mixed Berry Cobbler

- **1**   **package (16 ounces) frozen mixed berries**
- **¾**   **cup granulated sugar**
- **2**   **tablespoons quick-cooking tapioca**
- **2**   **teaspoons grated lemon peel**
- **1½**   **cups all-purpose flour**
- **½**   **cup packed brown sugar**
- **2¼**   **teaspoons baking powder**
- **¼**   **teaspoon ground nutmeg**
- **¾**   **cup reduced-fat (2%) milk**
- **2**   **tablespoons unsalted butter, melted**
-     **Vanilla ice cream or whipped cream (optional)**

Tip

Cobblers are year-round favorites. Experiment with seasonal fresh fruits, such as pears, plums, peaches, rhubarb, blueberries, raspberries, strawberries, blackberries or gooseberries. Also try different apple varieties such as Granny Smith, Fuji, Gala or a mix of your favorites.

1. Coat inside of **CROCK-POT®** slow cooker with nonstick cooking spray. Combine berries, granulated sugar, tapioca and lemon peel in medium bowl. Remove to **CROCK-POT®** slow cooker.

2. Combine flour, brown sugar, baking powder and nutmeg in medium bowl. Add milk and butter; stir just until blended. Drop spoonfuls of dough on top of berry mixture. Cover; cook on LOW 4 hours. Turn off heat. Uncover; let stand 30 minutes. Serve with ice cream, if desired.

Makes 8 servings

Nutrition Information: Serving Size ⅛ cobbler, Calories 228, Total Fat 3g, Saturated Fat 2g, Protein 3g, Carbohydrate 49g, Cholesterol 8mg, Dietary Fiber 2g, Sodium 111mg

Desserts

Fresh Berry Compote

- **2 cups fresh blueberries**
- **4 cups fresh sliced strawberries**
- **2 tablespoons orange juice**
- **½ cup sugar**
- **4 slices (1½ × ½ inches) lemon peel with no white pith**
- **1 cinnamon stick** *or* **½ teaspoon ground cinnamon**

Tip

To turn this compote into a fresh-fruit topping for cake, ice cream, waffles or pancakes, carefully spoon out fruit, leaving cooking liquid in **CROCK-POT®** slow cooker. Stir ¼ cup cold water into 1 to 2 tablespoons cornstarch in small bowl until smooth. Whisk into cooking liquid. Cover; cook on HIGH 15 minutes or until thickened. Return fruit to sauce; stir to blend.

1. Place blueberries in **CROCK-POT®** slow cooker. Cover; cook on HIGH 45 minutes or until blueberries begin to soften.

2. Add strawberries, orange juice, sugar, lemon peel and cinnamon stick; stir to blend. Cover; cook on HIGH 1 to 1½ hours or until berries soften and sugar dissolves.

3. Remove insert from **CROCK-POT®** slow cooker; let cool before serving.

Makes 4 servings

Nutrition Information: Serving Size about 1½ cups fruit and sauce, Calories 214, Total Fat 1g, Saturated Fat 0g, Protein 2g, Carbohydrate 55g, Cholesterol 0mg, Dietary Fiber 7g, Sodium 4mg

Classic Baked Apples

¼ cup packed dark brown sugar

2 tablespoons golden raisins

1 teaspoon grated lemon peel

6 medium baking apples, cored

1 teaspoon ground cinnamon

2 tablespoons unsalted butter, cubed

¼ cup water

¼ cup orange juice

Whipped cream (optional)

1. Combine brown sugar, raisins and lemon peel in small bowl; stir to blend. Fill core of each apple with mixture. Place apples in **CROCK-POT®** slow cooker. Sprinkle with cinnamon; dot with butter. Pour water and orange juice over apples. Cover; cook on LOW 7 to 9 hours or on HIGH 2½ to 3½ hours.

2. To serve, place apples in individual bowls. Top with sauce. Garnish with whipped cream, if desired.

Makes 6 servings

Nutrition Information: Serving Size 1 apple, Calories 180, Total Fat 4g, Saturated Fat 2g, Protein 1g, Carbohydrate 38g, Cholesterol 10mg, Dietary Fiber 5g, Sodium 6mg

Desserts

Peach Cobbler

2 packages (16 ounces *each*) frozen peaches, thawed and drained

¾ cup plus 1 tablespoon sugar, divided

2 teaspoons ground cinnamon, divided

½ teaspoon ground nutmeg

¾ cup all-purpose flour

2 tablespoons unsalted butter, melted

Whipped cream (optional)

Tip

To make cleanup easier when cooking sticky or sugary foods, spray the inside of the **CROCK-POT®** slow cooker with nonstick cooking spray before adding ingredients.

1. Combine peaches, ¾ cup sugar, 1½ teaspoons cinnamon and nutmeg in medium bowl; stir to blend. Remove to **CROCK-POT®** slow cooker.

2. Combine flour, remaining 1 tablespoon sugar and remaining ½ teaspoon cinnamon in small bowl. Drizzle with melted butter; toss to coat. Sprinkle over peach mixture. Cover; cook on HIGH 2 hours. Serve with whipped cream, if desired.

Makes 6 servings

Nutrition Information: Serving Size ⅙ cobbler, Calories 189, Total Fat 3g, Saturated Fat 7g, Protein 2g, Carbohydrate 41g, Cholesterol 8mg, Dietary Fiber 2g, Sodium 1mg

Desserts

Poached Pears with Raspberry Sauce

4 cups cranberry-apple-raspberry juice cocktail

2 cups Riesling wine

¼ cup sugar

2 cinnamon sticks, broken into halves

5 firm Bosc or Anjou pears, peeled

1 package (10 ounces) frozen raspberries in syrup, thawed

Fresh berries (optional)

Sprigs fresh mint (optional)

1. Combine juice cocktail, wine, sugar and cinnamon stick halves in **CROCK-POT®** slow cooker. Submerge pears in mixture. Cover; cook on LOW 3½ to 4 hours or until pears are tender. Remove and discard cinnamon stick halves.

2. Add raspberries to food processor or blender; process until smooth. Strain and discard seeds. Spoon raspberry sauce evenly onto serving plates; place pears on top of sauce. Garnish with fresh berries and mint.

Makes 5 servings

Nutrition Information: Serving Size 1 pear and ¼ cup sauce, Calories 390, Total Fat 0g, Saturated Fat 0g, Protein 1g, Carbohydrate 86g, Cholesterol 0mg, Dietary Fiber 7g, Sodium 35mg

Apple-Date Crisp

6 cups thinly sliced peeled Golden Delicious apples (about 6 medium)

2 teaspoons lemon juice

⅓ cup chopped dates

1⅓ cups quick oats

½ cup all-purpose flour

½ cup packed brown sugar

½ teaspoon ground cinnamon

¼ teaspoon ground ginger

¼ teaspoon salt

Dash ground nutmeg

Dash ground cloves (optional)

2 tablespoons unsalted butter, melted

1. Coat inside of **CROCK-POT®** slow cooker with nonstick cooking spray. Place apples in medium bowl. Sprinkle with lemon juice; toss to coat. Add dates; mix well. Remove mixture to **CROCK-POT®** slow cooker.

2. Combine oats, flour, brown sugar, cinnamon, ginger, salt, nutmeg and cloves, if desired, in medium bowl; stir to blend. Drizzle with butter; toss to blend. Sprinkle oat mixture over apples. Cover; cook on LOW 4 hours or on HIGH 2 hours or until apples are tender.

Makes 6 servings

Nutrition Information: Serving Size ⅙ crisp, Calories 252, Total Fat 4g, Saturated Fat 2g, Protein 3g, Carbohydrate 53g, Cholesterol 8mg, Dietary Fiber 6g, Sodium 178mg

Cherry Rice Pudding

1½ cups milk

1 cup hot cooked rice

3 eggs, beaten

½ cup sugar

¼ cup dried cherries or cranberries

½ teaspoon almond extract

¼ teaspoon salt

1 cup water

Ground nutmeg (optional)

1. Spray 1½-quart casserole with nonstick cooking spray. Combine milk, rice, eggs, sugar, cherries, almond extract and salt in large bowl. Pour into prepared casserole; stir to blend. Cover with buttered foil, butter side down.

2. Place rack in **CROCK-POT®** slow cooker and pour in water. Place casserole on rack. Cover; cook on LOW 4 to 5 hours.

3. Remove casserole from **CROCK-POT®** slow cooker. Let stand 15 minutes before serving. Garnish with nutmeg.

Makes 6 servings

Nutrition Information: Serving Size about ³/₄ cup, Calories 193, Total Fat 4g, Saturated Fat 1g, Protein 6g, Carbohydrate 33g, Cholesterol 111mg, Dietary Fiber 1g, Sodium 162mg

Desserts

Warm Spiced Apples and Pears

2 **tablespoons unsalted butter**

1 **cup packed brown sugar**

½ **cup water**

½ **lemon, sliced**

1 **teaspoon vanilla**

1 **cinnamon stick, broken in half**

½ **teaspoon ground cloves**

5 **pears, quartered and cored**

5 **small Granny Smith apples, cored and quartered**

Tip

Simmer a sweet treat in your CROCK-POT® slow cooker during dinner, so you can delight your family and guests with a delicious warm dessert.

1. Melt butter in saucepan over medium heat. Add brown sugar, water, lemon slices, vanilla, cinnamon stick halves and cloves. Bring to a boil; cook and stir 1 minute. Remove from heat.

2. Combine pears, apples and butter mixture in **CROCK-POT®** slow cooker; mix well. Cover; cook on LOW 3½ to 4 hours or on HIGH 2 hours, stirring every 45 minutes. Remove and discard cinnamon stick halves.

Makes 8 servings

Nutrition Information: Serving Size about 1¼ cups fruit and sauce, Calories 246, Total Fat 3g, Saturated Fat 2g, Protein 1g, Carbohydrate 58g, Cholesterol 8mg, Dietary Fiber 6g, Sodium 11mg

Pumpkin-Cranberry Custard

1 can (30 ounces) pumpkin pie filling

1 can (12 ounces) evaporated milk

1 cup dried cranberries

4 eggs, beaten

1 cup crushed or whole gingersnap cookies (optional)

Whipped cream (optional)

Combine pumpkin, evaporated milk, cranberries and eggs in **CROCK-POT®** slow cooker; mix thoroughly. Cover; cook on HIGH 4 to 4½ hours. Serve with gingersnaps and whipped cream, if desired.

Makes 8 servings

Nutrition Information: Serving Size about ¾ cup, Calories 267, Total Fat 5g, Saturated Fat 3g, Protein 8g, Carbohydrate 60g, Cholesterol 16mg, Dietary Fiber 13g, Sodium 392mg

Index

Index

Index

Index

Index

Index

Index

Metric Conversion Chart

VOLUME MEASUREMENTS (dry)

$1/8$ teaspoon = 0.5 mL
$1/4$ teaspoon = 1 mL
$1/2$ teaspoon = 2 mL
$3/4$ teaspoon = 4 mL
1 teaspoon = 5 mL
1 tablespoon = 15 mL
2 tablespoons = 30 mL
$1/4$ cup = 60 mL
$1/3$ cup = 75 mL
$1/2$ cup = 125 mL
$2/3$ cup = 150 mL
$3/4$ cup = 175 mL
1 cup = 250 mL
2 cups = 1 pint = 500 mL
3 cups = 750 mL
4 cups = 1 quart = 1 L

VOLUME MEASUREMENTS (fluid)

1 fluid ounce (2 tablespoons) = 30 mL
4 fluid ounces ($1/2$ cup) = 125 mL
8 fluid ounces (1 cup) = 250 mL
12 fluid ounces ($1 1/2$ cups) = 375 mL
16 fluid ounces (2 cups) = 500 mL

WEIGHTS (mass)

$1/2$ ounce = 15 g
1 ounce = 30 g
3 ounces = 90 g
4 ounces = 120 g
8 ounces = 225 g
10 ounces = 285 g
12 ounces = 360 g
16 ounces = 1 pound = 450 g

DIMENSIONS

$1/16$ inch = 2 mm
$1/8$ inch = 3 mm
$1/4$ inch = 6 mm
$1/2$ inch = 1.5 cm
$3/4$ inch = 2 cm
1 inch = 2.5 cm

OVEN TEMPERATURES

250°F = 120°C
275°F = 140°C
300°F = 150°C
325°F = 160°C
350°F = 180°C
375°F = 190°C
400°F = 200°C
425°F = 220°C
450°F = 230°C

BAKING PAN AND DISH EQUIVALENTS

Utensil	Size in Inches	Size in Centimeters	Volume	Metric Volume
Baking or Cake Pan (square or rectangular)	8×8×2	20×20×5	8 cups	2 L
	9×9×2	23×23×5	10 cups	2.5 L
	13×9×2	33×23×5	12 cups	3 L
Loaf Pan	8½×4½×2½	21×11×6	6 cups	1.5 L
	9×9×3	23×13×7	8 cups	2 L
Round Layer Cake Pan	8×1½	20×4	4 cups	1 L
	9×1½	23×4	5 cups	1.25 L
Pie Plate	8×1½	20×4	4 cups	1 L
	9×1½	23×4	5 cups	1.25 L
Baking Dish or Casserole			1 quart/4 cups	1 L
			1½ quart/6 cups	1.5 L
			2 quart/8 cups	2 L
			3 quart/12 cups	3 L